BRYAN WHITEFIELD

"I first worked with Bryan back in the early days of the COVID pandemic, when the spectre of the unknown loomed large. He brought frameworks for managing risk and making complex strategic decisions in a situation that was the very definition of the Uncertainty Paradox. *Team Think* offers practical and rigorous tools for all leaders as they embrace uncertainty, navigate complexity, and strive for the flow that underpins success."

– Ian Brooksbank, CEO, Hydro Tasmania

"As always, Bryan's book *Team Think* provides insights into how to put theory into practice. Decision making is one of the most difficult aspects to get right in organisations. It's impressive to see how Bryan effectively integrates various theories into a cohesive, systematic approach for navigating team decisions. As a risk professional, better team decision making is one of the keys to success."

– Keith Drayton, Chief Risk Officer, Reserve Bank of Australia

"Bryan takes us on a whirlwind tour of why and how team decision making can improve outcomes. He presents a range of models and ideas that allow the reader to consider different approaches. Perhaps applying some of the tools suggested in this book, readers can decide how to improve their decision making. An important reminder that with mindful application and design, together we can go further than trying to outthink the problem on our own."

– Scott Langford, Group CEO, St George Community Housing

"*Team Think* offers a fresh, transformative way to boost team performance. Bryan shows how to clear obstacles and leverage diverse perspectives, elevating team success. This book will inspire you to create an environment where top performers excel, leading to greater productivity and results."

– *Matt Paterson, Mayor, Alice Springs Town Council*

"*Team Think* is the pocket guide to getting your team humming. Full of practical advice, Bryan uses his engaging style to pull together the research and his own experience into an operating manual for leaders, to optimise team decision making."

– *Claudia Bels FAICD, Non-Executive Director, Audit & Risk Committee Chair*

"*Team Think* dives right into the heart of what makes or breaks team decisions and comes out with some serious gold. Bryan Whitefield has a way of breaking down the nitty-gritty of strategic planning and decision hygiene that's both eye-opening and, dare I say, fun. It's like having a chat with a wise friend who knows just how to steer your team to greatness. With insights on everything from leadership roles to tackling biases, this book is a must-have for anyone ready to lead their team to new heights. It's not just another business book; it's your team's next step to becoming unstoppable."

– *Donna McGeorge, Global Authority on Productivity and Best-Selling Author*

"Over the years, I've dedicated considerable thought to enhancing the speed and quality of team decision-making. Bryan's exceptional book thoughtfully explores the dynamics of team decision making, offering practical methods for optimising team decisions. Drawing from his extensive background in business, consulting and facilitation, Bryan provides compelling examples of how to use the optimisation process and create the right environment for faster and better team decisions."

— *Grahame Petersen, Director, Mary MacKillop Today and Redlands School, former Group Executive at CBA*

"*Team Think: How Teams Make Great Decisions* by Bryan Whitefield is essential for anyone involved in organisational leadership and decision-making. Bryan's expertise in linking decision-making processes with risk management is evident throughout the book. He masterfully demonstrates how effective decision-making enhances organisational performance and mitigates risk by fostering a culture of informed and collaborative decision-making. This book provides invaluable insights and practical tools that empower teams to navigate complex challenges with confidence and agility. It is a must-read for leaders who strive to make sound decisions that drive success and sustainability."

— *Simon Levy, CEO, Risk Management Institute of Australasia*

"Bryan has once again provided invaluable insights not just for the risk community, but for the broader business world. His guidance on key considerations and learnings is essential for building resilience. Risk management is about our people, and his book *Team Think* offers numerous practical and immediate takeaways that can be applied to strengthen our organisations moving forward."

– *David Turner, CEO, RiskNZ*

"Why do so many teams struggle with decision-making? As one of Australia's leading risk experts, Bryan understands the importance of culture and leadership better than most. Bryan's latest book, *Team Think*, explores Decision Flow in teams in a practical way with actionable insights for leaders. If you want to shift how your leaders and teams decide, *Team Think* is a must read."

– *Meredith Wilson, Culture Strategist, Executive Mentor and Author of* Shift: Everyday Actions Leaders Can Take to Shift Culture

"When teams are prepared - whether in sport or business - their success is seldom a stroke of luck. The only way to be prepared is to do the hard yards up front, and unfortunately, because they are 'hard yards', too many teams don't do this … resulting in costly consequences. This is why you need to invest the time to read and re-read this book *Team Think*."

– *Tim Sole, Retired Chief Executive, Ex CEO Asteron, Ex CEO Public Trust, Ex CEO State Insurance and Ex CEO Civic Assurance*

"As someone who is passionate about the value of high performing teams, it was refreshing to read Bryan Whitefield's *Team Think*. The book does a fantastic job of recognising the inherent complexity of teams and the environment they operate within, at the same time as offering a range of applicable frameworks and principles all designed to enable better decision making.

Readers and teams who apply the lessons of this book will make better decisions and that is a good thing for all of us."

– Keegan Luiters, Team Performance Expert:
Author, Speaker, Coach and Facilitator

"*Team Think* is a book that I strongly recommend to anyone involved in decision making, whether it be a board member, a member of an executive leadership team, management or just those required to make good decisions. The book is informative, thought provoking and an enjoyable read for a wide audience. Brian has a knack for making the complex simple to understand and peppers the text with tools to use in decision making, with examples that have relevance to a wide spectrum of readers.

Bryan spells out why decision making is critical to good organisational governance and the deficiencies in many organisations' governance frameworks around decision making. He highlights the cost to an organisation from poor decisions and why there is a need to focus attention, not only on the large "strategic" and "big bet" decisions at the start of a project, but equally importantly on the myriads of subsequent decisions, some big but many small, that are essential to successful execution of projects. He highlights the importance of good decision flow on an organisation's growth trajectory. What is needed to make quality team decisions quickly and provides a useful matrix to classify decisions so that the correct process can be identified for each decision.

His book is well referenced to the literature on decision making that supports his analysis but presents it in a coherent form that makes the complex research undertaken into the subject of decision making, easily absorbed by the reader.

Lastly, Bryan provides a wealth of experience in building support tools and processes for decision making. This is a "how to" book which I recommend as an essential read for those interested in decision making."

– *Stuart Black, Non-Executive Director, AACO, Noumi Limited*

"*Team Think* reflects a simple, practical philosophy with steps designed to develop decision flow throughout organisations and teams.

My profession is highly rank-structured, 'what the boss says goes' – this is both an advantage and a curse if a leader is not aware of how power imbalance impacts team decision making. Influence of the 'HiPPO (Highest Paid Person's Opinion)' must attract patience or risk the suppression of ideas and expressions of perspective. According to *Team Think*, 'even though a team leader may have the final say, a lot happens along the way that can influence the decision made.'

In policing we have a powerful purpose - keeping people and communities safe. The importance of sharing and iterating a purpose of meaning to drive motivation must be a central tenet of modern-day policing. Purpose attracts the right people and promotes the right approach in a labour market of increasing competition.

In policing, decision making models aligned with Bryan's principles are now embedded in operational preparation.

Decision trees assist police officers by guiding thinking about risk, promoting cooperative discussion and providing for collaborative decision making.

Perhaps my favourite quote is from the chapter 'Vibrant Veracity' where "some decision support tools … turn a decision from the gut feel of a gambler to considered risk taking." This has been my experience to ensuring safer policing, where acceptance of uncertainty does not mark the end of a decision making journey to develop greater clarity.

Policing cannot be effective without teamwork, and dare I say it, *Team Think*. Effective policing is not an individual undertaking. Success relies on the coordination of teams and decisions within a strong hierarchical culture. The promotion of teamwork alone is not enough. Aspects of *Team Think* must be considered, both strategically and tactically, to address and operate in an environment of increasing danger and volatility."

– Tony Crandell, Former Assistant Commissioner,
Technology Command, NSW Police Force

Team Think

Other books by the author:

Risky Business: How Successful Organisations Embrace Uncertainty

Persuasive Advising: How to Turn Red Tape into Blue Ribbon

Bryan's Blogs: From Blog to Book Years of Insights on Making Risk Stick

DECIDE: How to Manage the Risk in Your Decision Making

TEAM THINK

HOW TEAMS MAKE GREAT DECISIONS

BRYAN WHITEFIELD

Published by Bryan Whitefield Consulting
PO Box 7367 Warringah Mall
Brookvale NSW 2100 Australia

www.bryanwhitefield.com

First published 2024

Copyright © 2024 Bryan Whitefield

Bryan Whitefield asserts the moral right to be identified as the author of this work.

All rights reserved. No part of this publication may be reproduced, stored in a retrieval system or transmitted in any form or by any means, electronic, mechanical, photocopying, recording or otherwise, without the prior written permission of the publisher.

ISBN: 9781763529007

 A catalogue record for this book is available from the National Library of Australia

Cover design by Tim Denmead
Edited by Jem Bates
Typesetting by BookPOD
Printed by IngramSpark

About the author

Bryan Whitefield is a management consultant assisting organisations to unlock the secrets of high performance through a decision-making lens. He sees an organisation as, in its essence, simply people making decisions to act or not act in pursuit of the organisation's purpose.

Bryan's interest in decision making in organisations, particularly in the context of teams, should come as no surprise. After all, people are complex, and people interacting in teams are more complex … and he is fascinated by complexity. This fascination drew him to a career as a chemical engineer, which soon became a journey of exploration into decision making. It started with risk-based decision making, evolved into a keen interest in influencing the decisions of others, and culminated in a dedicated focus on team decision making, creating a beautiful flow of sound decision making in organisations of all shapes and sizes.

Bryan is the author of *Risky Business: How Successful Organisations Embrace Uncertainty* (Amazon Best Seller); *Bryan's Blogs: From Blog to Book — Years of Insights on Making Risk Stick* (Amazon Best Seller) and *Persuasive Advising: How to Turn Red Tape into Blue Ribbon*. He has worked with thousands of senior leaders and their teams across all sectors and was President and Chair of the Risk Management Institution of Australasia from 2013 through 2015.

Acknowledgements

You can't write a book on team decision making without being part of a team. My number one team is my family — my beautiful, loving wife, Jacquie, and my pride and joy Doug, Ben and Emily. What fun we have had as we have grown together, and what experiences we have had making our team decisions!

My second team for *Team Think* is my work team. Paula and Wendy are key cogs in the mechanics that push this practice along. In the later stages of writing this book, one cog had to be taken out of action. Congratulations, Paula, on the birth of Jared, your second child! We other cogs missed you and I learned another valuable lesson about teams and decision making: you don't know what you don't know. Fortunately the wonderful Wendy, Jacquie and I fuddled our way through, and here we are with my third book in a trilogy on decision making. And one I am very proud of.

To all my other teams of friends, colleagues, sporting teammates and the effervescent tribe at Thought Leaders Business School, you have taught me so much about operating as a team.

My final and gracious thanks go to all those wonderful clients within the client organisations I have served who I teamed up with to assist their team decisions in delivering mutual success. I hope I have honoured you with the concepts, tools and techniques I offer up to the world in this book.

Who should read this book?

Dare I say it . . .?

Everyone.

Sounds like hyperbole, does it not? Yet who is not part of a team of some description at some point in their lives. Even if only a team of two in a family or romantic relationship or simply a friendship. That means everyone on the planet who has come of age could do with some help in managing collective decisions.

Who is this book really for? The answer is:

- **Board Chairs** who crave good information flow to feel confident making decisions in oversight of organisations and who want to create an optimal environment for the board's deliberation on critical decisions.
- **Non-Executive Directors** who want to participate in collective decisions that matter and help their boards get decisions right.
- **Chief Executives** who want to lead their organisation at greater speed, especially those who want or need to make big-bet decisions.

- **Executives** and **team leaders** who want a smoother flow of decisions to them and from them to higher delegations. Only necessary decisions come to you and you are clear on the ones to escalate. Once those you escalate have been deliberated on, you are informed of the outcome or kept informed as deliberations continue.
- **Team members** who aspire to be better team members or to become team leaders. We are, after all, defined by the decisions we make!

Contents

Preface	xvii
Introduction	1

PART 1: TEAM DECISION MAKING

1 Not 'me', but 'we', is the problem — 7
- Making strategic decisions — 9
  - Strategic planning days — 11
  - Groupthink — 14
- Team recurring decisions — 16
- It's complex, not complicated — 18
- My declaration for *Team Think* — 21
- Chapter summary — 23

2 The value of team decision making — 25
- How teams make decisions — 29
  - Purpose — 31
  - Talent — 33
  - Connectedness — 35
- The drivers of flow — 36
- Chapter summary — 40

PART 2: FASTER, BETTER DECISION MAKING

3 Creating flow — 43
- Chapter summary — 50

4 Categorically critical — 51
- Kahneman — 52
- Bezos and Branson — 52

	McKinsey – De Smet, Lackey and Weiss	53
	Snowden	54
	Whitefield	56
	Time critical	58
	Chapter summary	59
5	**Delicate design**	61
	Collaboration	64
	Collation	65
	Clarification	72
	Chapter summary	73
6	**Vibrant veracity**	75
	Decision trees	76
	Multi-criteria decision analysis (MCDA)	79
	Risk assessment	81
	Risk appetite	83
	Anonymous voting	84
	Data models	86
	Visualising data	87
	Chapter summary	89

PART 3: STRATEGIC OR BIG-BET DECISIONS

7	**Go mental**	93
	Mental modelling	94
	Building narratives	100
	Chapter summary	103
8	**Go hard**	105
	Developing meta-mental models	106
	Overlaps, contradictions and trade-offs	108

	Shifts and blind spots	109
	Your meta-mental model	111
	Chapter summary	114
9	**Go fast**	115
	Hot LIPS	117
	Gates	120
	Signals	122
	Doubling down	124
	Chapter summary	126

PART 4: DECISION HYGIENE

10	**The unmaking of strategic decisions**	131
	Common types of bias	133
	Organisational bias	135
	Common factors causing noise	136
	Chapter summary	138
11	**Leading by asking**	141
	The Why Model	143
	Implementation	144
	Clarification	144
	Motivation	145
	The Drivers Model	147
	The Think Model	149
	The Player Model	151
	Allows effective processing	152
	Resistant to triggers	152
	Avoidance of bias	152
	Chapter summary	153
12	**Role play**	155

	Chair of the Board	155
	Commander-in-Chief	158
	Command and control environments	158
	Ministerial environments	158
	Advisory boards or committees	159
	Chief Risk Officer	159
	Chief Safety Officer	162
	Chief Cynic	163
	Chapter summary	165
13	**Think like Einstein**	167
	Chapter summary	170
	The wrap	171
	Endnotes	173

List of figures

Figure 1: Human error rates	14
Figure 2: Decision value curve	27
Figure 3: Decision flow	28
Figure 4: Quality of team decisions	30
Figure 5: Decision landscapes	39
Figure 6: Creating flow	49
Figure 7: Decision categorisation matrix	56
Figure 8: Mental model mapping process	63
Figure 9: Sample decision process map	69
Figure 10: Sample decision tree for incident response	77
Figure 11: Sample decision tree for allocating risk in a contract	78
Figure 12: Sample MCDA for permit application	79
Figure 13: Sample MCDA for supplier selection	79
Figure 14: Sample risk scoring tool	82
Figure 15: Example of visualisation of data (Source: PowerSlides)	88
Figure 16: Meta-mental models	107
Figure 17: Quadrant Planning Model	119
Figure 18: The Strategy Funnel Mk II	122
Figure 19: The Why Model	143
Figure 20: The Drivers Model	148

Figure 21: The Think Model — 150

Figure 22: The Player Model — 151

Figure 23: Psychological Safety — 163

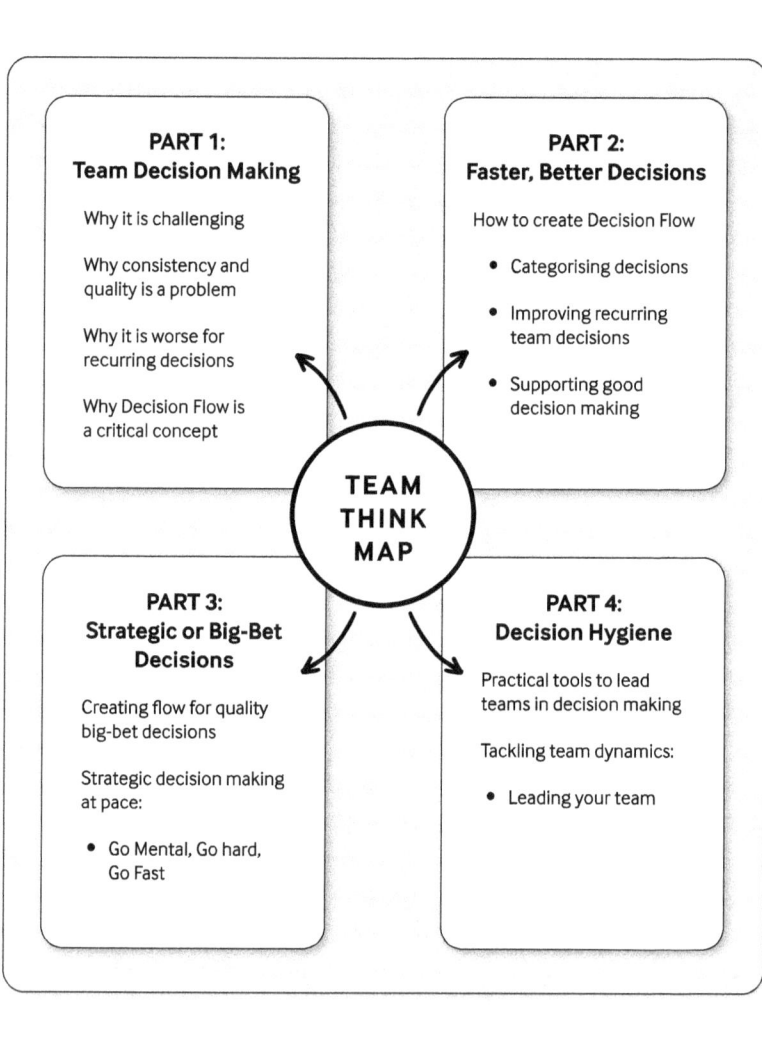

Preface

I am a passionate thinker and have found deep thinking the best way to get the most out of life without regret. As a young adult I was good at thinking things through even when it came to my social life — paaaarrrtttyyy! My enthusiastic, impatient friends would often jump at the first opportunity to party. Not me. I would check the options available, consider who would likely be there and the atmosphere to expect, and appraise the logistics, pre mobile phones, of getting there and getting home again! Many times I was first taunted and later praised for taking the time to think those things through. I guess I have always been thinking one way or another about decision making, in particular, team decision making.

Many years ago, the way I thought about decision making, in organisations in particular, underwent a massive shift. After I read Herbert A. Simon's *Administrative Behaviour*, originally published in the 1940s, I became convinced that improving decision-making skills and processes was the answer to overcoming so many challenges and grasping so many opportunities. Simon explained how, once the purpose of an organisation is established, all that remains is for management to influence decision making to ensure the most appropriate actions are taken by those within the organisation to fulfil its purpose. Simon proposed that a perfect decision is one in which all possible consequences are foreseen. Of course, in the real world there is no such luxury. Not all consequences are foreseeable. And throughout my career I have witnessed first-hand the positive results of very good decision making and, conversely, the negative outcomes of poor decisions.

After graduating from the University of Sydney I started my career as a chemical engineer. I chose 'chem-eng' after a tour of the engineering department at an open day because it fascinated me the most. What attracted me was its complexity — the fact that I had little or no clue as to what was happening inside the lab-sized glass distillation column, where mysterious fluids bubbled and splashed and were drawn off by exit pipes at different heights. Far from being daunted by these mysteries, I simply had to find out more.

Across my engineering career I learned that the chemical industry is indeed complex, but the industry had devised ways of managing that complexity. They had ways of representing entire plants on paper using piping and instrument diagrams. They had chemistry for describing, in simple terms, what was happening inside a reactor. Despite the best efforts of the industry, people still made mistakes and those mistakes could be catastrophic. Many hundreds, sometimes thousands, were killed in accidents. And this risk persists to this day.

After running chemical plants, I moved into the world of insuring them and pretty much any other industry. I found myself at CE Heath, which eventually became HIH Insurance. I watched from within its meteoric rise to become one of Australia's largest international insurers, only to see it fall even more dramatically in Australia's largest ever corporate collapse. I learned a lot about decision making and how leaders' decisions change as their circumstances change.

High-risk industries such as the insurance industry and the chemical industry were leaders in developing methods for making decisions where there was a high degree of uncertainty. I learned these skills and from the mid 1990s started to bring them into the even more complex world of businesses such as hospitals, aged care facilities, disability services, tech companies and many, many others.

Why is the business world more complex? Because of people. In the chemical industry, many of the decisions are bound by the laws of physics and chemistry. As I developed my business facilitation skills, I had more and more opportunities to help executives make some of the most important decisions for their organisations and for their careers. All the time I was learning about the art of decision making. In particular, team decision making.

I read, I researched and I contemplated. Team decision making is tough, and the risks are well documented by the likes of Kahneman, Tversky, Lovallo, Sibony, Sunstein, Hastie, Thaler, Plous, Gigerenzer, Nutt, Chiles and more. But it seemed to me something was missing from the literature and from the real world of decision making. In time, the missing pieces of the puzzle became clear to me, and I felt compelled to share these insights.

In this book I articulate for you the challenges posed by team decision making and provide you with methodologies for improving decision making across your organisation to create a wonderful flow of decisions. Decisions that will ensure your organisation's performance is outstanding and the envy of your industry.

Introduction

We are all fallible. We all get decisions wrong from time to time. Worse still, once we have made bad decisions and formed strong beliefs, we struggle to overturn them. As Professor Scott Galloway writes, 'Your decisions are a guide and an action plan, not a suicide pact.'[1]

Fortunately we now have 50 years of research in the behavioural sciences — backed by the work of Nobel Prize winners Daniel McFadden in 2000, George Akerlof in 2001, Daniel Kahneman in 2002, Thomas Schelling in 2005 and Robert Shiller in 2013 — that outlines the challenges we have with decision making and a range of ideas on how to overcome them.[2]

The problem is there are so many issues and solutions, it's difficult to know where to start or what to do next. And we seem to get by just fine even if we don't get every decision 100 per cent correct. After all, how else did we get to where we are now if we were not pretty good at decision making?

It's hard to argue that point. However, whenever I make statements on the challenges of team decision making, I always get enthusiastic nods of agreement.

Given this state of affairs I have included in this book as much practical advice as I could muster for you to implement what you need for your organisation to thrive.

I have structured this book into four parts. Part 1 introduces team decision making. In chapter 1 I delve into some of its challenges, explore the research and recognise the complexity of team discussions. In chapter 2 I put into perspective the value of team decisions and compare the value of a strategic decision with the value of the many thousands of team decisions made in execution of that decision. *Hint: all team decisions matter!* I also prescribe the mix of attributes a team needs to thrive at team decision making and I introduce the concept of *decision flow* in organisations, where *flow* is a wonderful mix of fast and high-quality decisions.

Part 2 outlines how to create flow. In chapter 3 I build the case for flow and set the scene for chapters 4 through 6, where I take you through the three core elements you will need to be across: categorising decisions, designing good processes for decision flow and designing decision support tools to be used by leaders at critical points across various processes.

Part 3 is all about strategic or big-bet decisions. In chapter 7 I explore how we all have different mental models of the world in which we operate and how narratives are formed from mental models. In chapter 8 I take you through a process for blending individual narratives until you have a meta-mental model of the world the team can lean into. And in chapter 9 I introduce my process for strategy design so you can execute strategic decisions at pace and with minimal backtracking.

Part 4 is all about decision hygiene. Kahneman, Sibony and Sunstein used this term in their important book *Noise: A Flaw in Human Judgment* (2020) and I decided to run with it. But my aim here was to blend the findings and advice from such heavyweights with my own experience, and produce a range of practical tools to help you lead better team conversations, resulting in faster and better decisions. In chapter 10 I cover the sources of poor team decision making. In chapter 11 I provide four models to help you understand and tackle team dynamics and the personal traits of individuals in your team. In chapter 12 I explore how different roles, from Chair of the Board through to Chief Risk Officer, can influence team decision making in the most positive way. Finally, in chapter 13 I take Kahneman and associates' suggestion of a Decision Observer and explore it for you in a practical way.

> This is not an academic book. It is an operating manual.

As I hope I have made it clear, this is not an academic book. It is an operating manual. I humbly ride on the coat tails of the great authors in this field. (For full transparency, I stole that line from James Clear, author of *Atomic Habits*. ☺)

Part 1

Team decision making

1

Not 'me', but 'we', is the problem

Deciding where to have dinner in Paris this evening can be pretty straightforward if it is you making the decision and you've had a restaurant recommended by multiple people as a 'simply must go'. Now bring your partner into the process. Your partner has had a different restaurant recommended to them. Or perhaps the restaurant you would like to go to specialises in seafood and your partner is not too keen on seafood.

Now think about the journey to Paris. You suggested a family holiday in Europe. That was pretty easy to get agreement on as none of the kids had been. Next challenge was the itinerary. You wanted to spend more time in France, particularly in Paris, than did the rest of the family. You had to compromise.

This morning you woke up and, given it was a rainy day and the family had already visited the big guns like the Louvre, you suggested a visit to Notre Dame Cathedral. To your frustration, the kids much preferred a visit to a science museum like the Musée des Arts et Métiers with its historical collection of more than 2,000 scientific inventions.

> Making our own decisions is much more straightforward than making team decisions.

Making our own decisions is much more straightforward than making team decisions, including decisions made by the CEO, who is influenced by the executive team even in the most autocratic, command-and-control environment. And therein lies one of the most perplexing challenges of modern organisations. How do we make great decisions fast and see them through to a successful conclusion? And what is the cost if we fail? A 2018 McKinsey survey of top executives provides an indication:

> On average, respondents spend 37 percent of their time making decisions, and more than half of this time was thought to be spent ineffectively. For managers at an average Fortune 500 company, this could translate into more than 530,000 days of lost working time and roughly $250 million of wasted labor costs per year.[3]

Put another way, almost 20 per cent of any executive's time is wasted because of ineffective decision making! The good news is the researchers determined that high-performing organisations are ones with good decision-making practices.

Let's begin by exploring the symptoms of poor decisions before I expand your thinking on good practices.

We will start with strategic decisions, the most important of all, to identify how good or bad leaders of organisations have traditionally been. Then we will explore the kind of team decisions made frequently by team members: for example, insurance-claim managers deciding on a pay-out, government agencies deciding whether or not to issue a permit or sales managers forecasting sales to ensure sufficient stock is on hand to fulfil orders. I refer to these as recurring decisions, the term used by Daniel Kahneman, Olivier Sibony and Cass R. Sunstein in their 2021 book *Noise: A Flaw in Human Judgment*.

Making strategic decisions

Landing a man on the moon in 1969 was one of humankind's greatest achievements, yet it had its problems along the way. Three astronauts died, it cost way more than originally projected, and although NASA met the deadline President Kennedy set in 1961 to achieve this massive feat 'by the end of the decade', the entire project took much longer than planned.

So what is a successful strategic decision?

In his book *Why Decisions Fail*[4] Paul C. Nutt unpacks

decades of research into 400 decisions made by managers of organisations from a broad range of industries and from many countries. Many companies are household names in the US and worldwide, like AT&T, Disney and Ford. Nutt's criteria for judging a successful decision is whether the decision was 'put to use' and was sustained over at least two years. While any number of arguments could be made for a different set of criteria, Nutt's are tough but reasonable, given that these are strategic decisions.

Nutt found that more than half of management decisions fail. That is staggering, given the time, money and will put into making them. Yet, considering the uncertainty surrounding strategic decisions and the challenge of team decision making, is it any wonder the scoreboard reveals such a poor performance?

> A 2009 survey of more than 2,200 executives showed that '60 per cent thought that bad decisions were about as frequent as good ones.'

Perhaps Nutt's criteria are too harsh, I hear you say. Well, consider the opinions on the quality of strategic decision making from a survey of executives by consulting firm McKinsey & Company, as reported in an article by Dan Lovallo and Olivier Sibony.[5] A 2009 survey of more than 2,200 executives showed that 'only 28 per cent said that the quality of strategic decisions in their companies was generally good, 60 per cent thought that bad decisions were about as frequent as good ones, and the remaining 12 per cent thought good decisions were altogether infrequent.'

Not convinced yet? Let's look at some statistics provided in a *Harvard Business Review* article by Dan Lovallo and Daniel Kahneman. In 'Delusions of Success: How Optimism Undermines Executives' Decisions'[6] they point out:

> More than 70 percent of new manufacturing plants in North America, for example, close within their first decade of operation. Approximately three-quarters of mergers and acquisitions never pay off — the acquiring firm's shareholders lose more than the acquired firm's shareholders' gain. And efforts to enter new markets fare no better; the vast majority end up being abandoned within a few years.

What about more run-of-the-mill strategic decisions, like the ones made at strategic planning days? Maybe they are made a little better.

Strategic planning days

If you have ever been on a strategic planning day like the one I outline below, you won't be shocked by the statistics on decision making that follow:

- A day is set aside two months ahead of time and the invitations are sent out to the leadership team.
- About one month out an agenda of topics is provided with names beside each item.

- Individuals prepare their presentations.
- Someone takes care of logistics for the off-site meeting including the very important choice of a restaurant for dinner.
- The day arrives and starts with a pep talk. The agenda is confirmed and it is agreed how the outcomes of the session will be captured.
- The first presentation is engaging but runs a bit long and leaves the team hanging as to what decision needs to be made. What was the question?
- The second presentation goes over time as well so the third presentation starts after a shortened morning tea. The presenter speeds through and hits you with a recommendation without providing sufficient background, leaving the team with a sense of not having enough information to make an informed call. The decision is delayed until later in the day.
- Team building exercise.
- More presentations.
- Document actions and responsibilities.
- The wrap-up pep talk.

The end result is that you head back to work with all the problems you had before the planning day, together with a list of new actions to take.

What if a planning day is better organised and some real hard thinking and deciding are accomplished, with results to be built into a strategic plan? The plan will have plenty of background information, a host of graphs and statistics, competitor analysis and the SWOT matrix. It will include the vision statement, the strategic pillars, some strategic imperatives and a whole host of strategic initiatives. All wrapped up with a comprehensive list of key performance indicators (KPIs) for each initiative, imperative and pillar.

The result? A plan no one wants to wade through. A plan that people interpret for their area of the business as best they can, but that they can't be bothered to read through to understand what it all means. Reporting against the KPIs requires two people full-time for two weeks for each reporting period. And most of what is produced is not considered by management anyway.

Worse still, sometimes the new plan is the start of something fresh, big and exciting. In *Rework*, Jason Fried and David Heinemeier Hansson, the creators of the Basecamp project management phenomenon, suggest the worst possible time to make a detailed plan for a major initiative is at the beginning. That's when we know the least!

The decisions made on strategic planning days are not just complicated; they are complex. Figure 1 shows a few statistics from the 'human error assessment and reduction technique' developed by J. C. Williams.[7]

> The decisions made on strategic planning days are not just complicated; they are complex.

Decision	Probability of Error
Task that is unfamiliar, needs to be performed at speed, no idea of outcome	0.55
Complex task requiring high level of comprehension and skill	0.16
Routine, highly practised, rapid task involving relatively low level of skill	0.02
Totally familiar task, performed several times per hour, well-motivated, highly trained staff, time to correct errors	0.0004

Figure 1: Human error rates

Given a 16 per cent fail rate on complex tasks, let alone a complex strategic plan, it will come as no surprise that the best we can hope for is a 16 per cent fail rate and more likely something approaching the 50 per cent reported in the McKinsey survey. And there are the hideously wrong decisions that teams can make that are an effect of what is commonly referred to as groupthink.

Groupthink

The original concept of groupthink was developed in the early 1970s by Irving Janis in an attempt to understand high-profile decisions in the previous decade that, with the benefit of hindsight, were poor because they ignored the facts. Examples included decisions leading to the escalation of the Vietnam War and to the Bay of Pigs military action in Cuba. In a 1973 article, Janis outlines eight main symptoms of groupthink:[8]

1. An illusion of invulnerability, leading to extreme risk taking.
2. Collective efforts to rationalise, leading to ignoring warning signs.
3. Belief in their own morality, leading to ignoring ethical or moral consequences.
4. Stereotyped views of rivals, leading to disdaining dialogue with them and/or underestimating them.
5. Peer pressure to remain loyal, leading to dissenters being silenced.
6. Self-censorship, leading to unvoiced doubts and counterarguments.
7. A shared illusion of unanimity, leading to false assumptions that silence means consent.
8. Self-appointed 'mindguards', leading to blocking of adverse information reaching the group.

It's quite a collection, don't you think? Any one of them can lead to poor outcomes; collectively, they can result in disaster. However, in their book *Wiser: Getting Beyond Groupthink to Make Groups Smarter* (2014), Cass R. Sunstein and Reid Hastie reject the idea that any one set of characteristics can explain groupthink: 'other case studies (involving the Nixon White House and the launch of the Challenger space shuttle) do not support Janis's claims. Experimental research fails consistently to link particular group characteristics, including those that Janis emphasized, to groupthink'.

Sunstein and Hastie argue that Janis did not have the benefit of the decades of research in the behavioural sciences they bring to bear in their work: 'To date . . . no one has focused, in any sustained way, on how the recent behavioural findings bear on the performance of firms and other groups. We aim to fill that gap.'[9] They explain their findings on why group decision making fails and the methods they have identified for generating successful group decisions.

Okay. I'm sure you get that teams don't always make great strategic decisions. What about more day-to-day, recurring team decisions such as those made by a team of insurance underwriters or a government team deciding on which projects will receive funding?

Team recurring decisions

I referred earlier to *Noise: A Flaw in Human Judgment* (2021) by Daniel Kahneman, Olivier Sibony and Cass R. Sunstein for good reason. These authors have worked in the behavioural science fields for decades and are well aware of how personal and team bias come into play in team decision making. In *Noise*, they explain that errors in our decision making come from a combination of bias and what they call 'noise'.

Bias is a systematic error of judgement. A typical example might be a bias against statistics. Some leaders live by the dictum that there are three types of lies: 'lies, damned lies and statistics'.[10] They will consistently dismiss statistical evidence when it goes against their gut feelings. However, as Eric Bonabeau argues in 'Don't Trust Your Gut' in the

1: NOT 'ME', BUT 'WE', IS THE PROBLEM | 17

Harvard Business Review,[11] behavioural science provides evidence that going with your gut against well-prepared statistical analysis is a mistake.

Noise, on the other hand, refers to random effects on our decision making. Kahneman, Sibony and Sunstein provide multiple examples from differing medical opinions to decisions on whether to grant bail to a felon to interest-rate forecasting to reveal different people, presented with the same facts, decide differently. Just think of the different responses of government decision makers from different countries or from different jurisdictions within the same country on Covid-19, for instance!

It does not stop there for *Noise*. Not only will different people make different decisions, but the same person may also make a different decision on the same evidence at different times. Why? Because, like it or not, our decision making is affected by how we feel on the day. Kahneman et al. give multiple examples such as: '[J]udges have been found more likely to grant parole at the beginning of the day or after a food break than immediately before such a break. If judges are hungry, they are tougher.'[12]

> Like it or not, our decision making is affected by how we feel on the day.

Having spoken to many hundreds of people about team decision making, all of whom agree it is fraught with obstacles to optimum decisions, I acknowledge it is a challenge. Fortunately for you and me, Kahneman et al.

once again have done the heavy lifting to put some numbers to the scale of the problem. In a study of the noise associated with insurance underwriting, they calculated a median variability of 55 per cent. That is, one insurance underwriter might quote a price almost double another for the same client. And being a median variability, half the time the difference would have been even larger! The impact on the bottom line? According to Kahneman et al., 'One senior executive estimated that the company's annual cost of noise in underwriting — counting both the loss of business from excessive quotes and the losses incurred on under-priced contracts — was in the hundreds of millions of dollars.'[13]

To sum up the importance of tackling noise in team decision making, look no further than this quote from *Noise*: 'The topic of bias has been discussed in thousands of scientific articles and dozens of popular books, few of which even mention the issue of noise. This book is our attempt to redress the balance.'[14]

Now you understand the historic levels of systematic error in team decision making caused by bias and noise, I will help you explore why team decision making is so difficult.

It's complex, not complicated

A team is a micro-organisation within an organisation and organisations are more than just complicated; they are complex systems. Let me explain.

In her book *Complexity: A Guided Tour*, complex systems

scientist Melanie Mitchell provides a layperson's definition of complexity as 'a system in which large networks of components with no central control and simple rules of operation give rise to complex collective behaviour, sophisticated information processing, and adaptation via learning or evolution.' Think of the behaviour of a school of fish. They swim along in perfectly synchronised unison, somehow knowing when to turn left or right and where to locate food and shelter. When their complex system, the school, is disrupted by a predator, the school quickly disperses, only to regroup and continue once the threat is past. There is no leader, just a sort of mysterious collective consciousness.

This is important because human organisations are not complicated, but they are complex. The organisation, and each team within it, develops a form of collective consciousness that manifests in the organisation and its teams' culture. To understand the importance, you need look no further than this explanation by Aaron Dignan in his *Brave New Work* on 'Changing Organizational Mindset'.[15]

Dignan explains the difference between complicated and complex by comparing it to the difference between a car and traffic. A car is complicated. It has many components. A car with a combustion engine is powered by a chemical reaction that turns fuel into energy, and this process is also complicated. Yet everything about that car has been worked out by scientists and engineers. The individual components have been understood, linked together and arranged for a specific purpose: the movement of the vehicle.

Traffic also seems complicated. We have become better at understanding traffic flow but while we can predict what is likely to happen, no one has yet been able to predict its flow with enough certainty to be able to control it. Dignan makes the point that while we can work out cause and effect in a complicated system and therefore control it, we can only manage complex systems by nudging them. He explains that complex systems are more about 'relationships and interactions among their components than about the components themselves. And these interactions give rise to unpredictable behaviour.'

Another non-human example used to explain complex systems is an ant colony. Individual ants appear to behave quite erratically, heading in one direction then another, seemingly at random. As they encounter other ants, however, their behaviour starts to change. And as more and more ants interact, more and more 'teams' are formed to perform specific duties, such as building ant bridges to cross 'valleys' or defending the colony against attack. In other words, some form of collective consciousness emerges. Scientists describe an emergent system as one in which behaviours develop from the relationships and interactions between elements of the system. In the case of traffic, it is the interaction between vehicles.

This leads to Melanie Mitchell's alternative definition of a complex system as 'a system that exhibits nontrivial emergent and self-organising behaviours.' Take a moment to reflect on this definition and your perceptions of an organisation. In an organisation of any size, the leadership team imagines their strategies and decisions will be implemented in a certain way but rarely are they implemented exactly as anticipated. Some elements of self-organising behaviours emerge, and that is the essence of organisational culture — the way we do things around here.

This brings us to Dignan's point about organisations as complex systems: 'organizational culture isn't a problem to be solved; it's an emergent phenomenon that we have to cultivate.' It is impossible to control an organisation through policy, process and system, despite our best efforts. We end up with plenty of rules and constraints, and these create friction and organisational drag. The way to nurture the culture of an organisation, he argues, is to create the right conditions for individual decision makers to find a way to achieve organisational goals.

> It is impossible to control an organisation through policy, process and system, despite our best efforts.

Thanks, Aaron, but easier said than done! This has been my focus for decades and means I am true to one of my most interesting traits: I always choose the more challenging path in life — haha!

My declaration for *Team Think*

In the next chapter I will first help you consider the value of a decision before moving on to explore team decision making in more depth, drawing on the work of the authors of *Wiser* and *Noise* among others.

You may have noticed I have quoted the authors of *Wiser* and *Noise* on their declared intentions for their books. *Wiser* focuses on team decision making from the perspective of the behavioural sciences and *Noise* sets out to redress an imbalance in the discussion of bias, together with the failure to address the importance of noise in team decision making. Now it is time for me to declare my own aim for this book.

When I read *Noise* in late 2021 and *Wiser* in early 2022 I remarked to more than one person that my book *Team Think* (which I'd been researching since mid 2020) had already been written by researchers like Kahneman and Sunstein. I questioned what I could add to the work of such esteemed academics, researchers and authors. I reflected on my years of practical experience in assisting boards, executive leadership teams and other teams to make better decisions, and my experience of writing practical, helpful business books on decision making (*Risky Business*, on risk-based decision making, and *Persuasive Advising*, on influencing decision making), and I came to the conclusion that *Team Think* needed to be written.

And so, my declaration.

My aim is to provide you with a clear understanding of the dynamics of team decision making and how to implement practical methods to optimise them, so whether you are the Chair of the Board, the CEO, a team leader, a team member or a key adviser on decisions, such as the Chief Risk Officer, you can be a high-performance leader. A leader who unblocks bottlenecks, unlocks the value of the intelligence within a team, and makes faster and better decisions.

Chapter summary

Just as most people think they are good drivers, most people think they are good decision makers and everyone else has a problem. This is nowhere more in evidence than when a joint decision is required. While it might be easy for a family to agree on Europe as the next destination for a holiday, things become more difficult when it comes to agreeing on which countries to visit and which regions or cities within those countries and how long to spend in each. Then you arrive and have to agree on what to do each day! We have all experienced it.

> Just as most people think they are good drivers, most people think they are good decision makers and everyone else has a problem.

The same kinds of problems arise with team decisions; even though a team leader may have a final say, a lot happens along the way that can influence the decision made.

Research shows that too much time is wasted on decision making and that the bigger and more complex the decision, the less often teams get it right. Which means it should come as no surprise that research shows the best organisations are good at decision making.

My aim for this book is for it to be a practical guide to improving team decision making, whether they be one-off strategic decisions or decisions made on a recurring basis such as product pricing in the private sector, or which non-governmental organisation (NGO) to grant funding to in the public sector, or which grants to apply for in the not-for-profit (NFP) sector.

2

The value of team decision making

Before you can adequately identify the value of a decision, you need to get your head around valuing intangibles. I know, I know, it is difficult. However, we do have some very clear examples to guide us. One of the clearest and most famous is the story of Facebook.

On May 18, 2012, Mark Zuckerberg's Facebook was publicly listed for trading on the US stock exchange, with a market valuation in the vicinity of US$100 billion dollars. Impressive, isn't it? In fact, it was incredibly impressive as it was based on annualised earnings in the vicinity of just US$500 million. By February 19, 2014, Facebook's market capitalisation was of the order of US$170 billion when 2013 earnings were

> Before you can adequately identify the value of a decision, you need to get your head around valuing intangibles.

around US$2 billion. According to the NASDAQ, Facebook's 2013 price–earnings ratio was about 129,[16] compared with a prevailing PE average of about 20 for technology stocks.

Some way, somehow, investors figured that Facebook had the potential to grow its earnings to the extent it could return to shareholders $129 for $1 invested now. Or, to put it another way, the 'market' felt Zuckerberg, the board and management and staff, could collectively make the right decisions to justify their investment. There were no hard assets, no guaranteed revenue streams; there was simply a phenomenon that positioned Facebook in a new market segment, just as Amazon and Google had been positioned. Investors believed that somehow the team, with all that intellectual capital, would work out how to multiply future revenue streams many, many times.

Wind forward ten years and those investors have been proved right. Facebook Inc., now Meta Platforms Inc., which is the parent company of Facebook, Instagram, Messenger and WhatsApp, managed to deliver some spectacular returns for investors. If you had invested $10,000 in 2013, by 15 March 2023 you would have had over $66,000 in share value.[17] A return of more than six times. Given many people invest in property with the notion that a property doubles in value every ten years, doing better than 600 per cent is quite an investment.

So how important is a decision and how does the value of one big decision, made by you, compare with the value of decisions made by others later in a project? Let's think about the decision to expand capacity of an existing manufacturing process. Let's assume it will cost in the order of $100 million and will take at least 18 months from decision time until the first product from the expanded facility is shipped to market. The first decision, to expand the plant, is obviously the biggest one. However, once that decision is made, many thousands of decisions will need to be made by staff, contractors and suppliers before the plant is in full production. There will be decisions about technology and about which supplier to use. There will be decisions about the timing of purchases and modes of transport. There will be decisions about hiring additional plant operators and how best to train them. Are you getting the same feeling I am getting? The size and the importance of decisions is reducing over time, but their numbers are increasing (see figure 2).

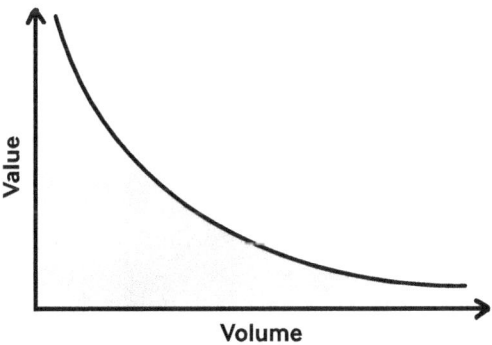

Figure 2: Decision value curve

If you are a bit of a mathematician, you will recognise figure 2 as an inverse exponential curve. The area under the curve, for any particular segment of the curve, depicts the value of a decision or decisions. The curve indicates a rapid rate of change along the vertical axis (the value axis) as you move along the horizontal axis (the volume of decisions) towards the tail of the curve. This means that although one or two decisions at the beginning of the curve have a huge potential value, by the tail of the curve their value will be the same as the thousands of subsequent decisions.

What does this mean for you? As shown in figure 3, it means you need good decision flow — that is, you had better get the big early decisions as right as possible, but it also means you had better have all your teams making good decisions along the way, given their sheer volume. And you want them making quality decisions with a minimum of effort to maximise organisational agility because this will impact your growth trajectory.

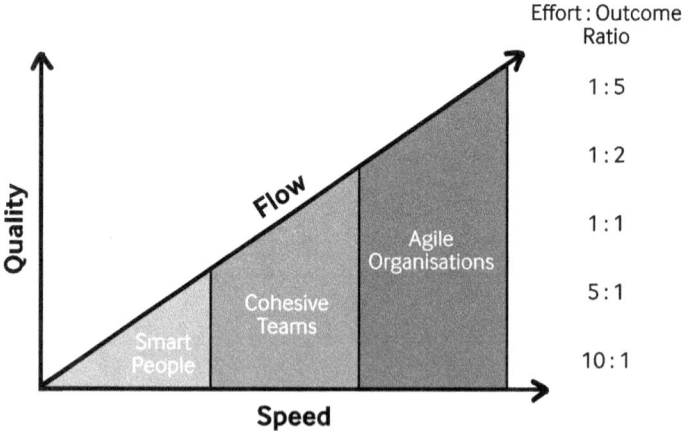

Figure 3: Decision flow

That's the value — but how to achieve that value? It starts with understanding the mechanics of team decision making under various scenarios.

How teams make decisions

Not too many years ago I was at a conference gala dinner in my black-tie penguin suit, chatting at the back of the room with a colleague from the private sector and another from the public sector. We were talking about a television comedy series called *Utopia*. The gist of the show is creating comedy from how decisions are made in a government agency called the National Building Authority. The comedy lies in how public servants, who wish to make decisions based on data and the public good, are constantly overruled by politicians.

I raised a recent episode involving a team meeting off-site for strategic planning. My colleague in the public service said he watched the episode just after returning from his own team's off-site and 'it was like they must have had cameras in our room!'

What can you take from this? Teams make decisions by following a process. That process may be informal or formal with specific guidelines; it may be good, bad or indifferent; it may be highly political; or it may be a process that inevitably ends up with the leader deciding, irrespective of how a proposition for the decision was put forward.

> Teams make decisions by following a process.

I've already insisted that decision flow needs decision quality. To have good quality, the process a team follows needs to score well in three key areas. Clarity of team *purpose*, the quality of the *talent* in the team and how *connected* team members feel (see figure 4). On the bottom rung of each ladder you will find a team whose purpose is blurred or whose members are plodders or are making decisions in isolation, and who can (and most likely will) reach decisions that are incorrect and require much reworking. This is crippling for the team as a whole.

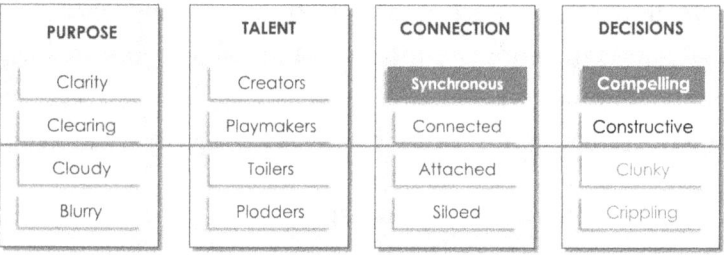

Figure 4: Quality of team decisions

On the next rung, you will see teams who will at best feel clunky as they are forced to expend excess effort just to get the job done. They can only glimpse their purpose through the clouds. They may be hard-working, task-oriented, join-the-dots toilers. Or perhaps consultation occurs only when team members are 'attached' to decisions — for example, when formal sign-offs are required.

Another rung up and you'll recognise many of the teams you are leading or have led in the past, and ones you have been a part of. They will have been quite constructive. They might not all have had absolute clarity of purpose, and some players may have done better than others, but it's likely some pretty strong relationships will have been built.

But how many of your teams are at the top of the ladder, making decisions that are compelling for them and for those around them? Decisions people feel compelled to support and deliver on? How many of them would give a 10/10 rating for clarity of their team's purpose? How many team members would you rate as creative? Not just problem solvers but true innovators? And how many in the team would say they feel completely in sync with others in making decisions?

Let's explore the role of *purpose*, *talent* and *connectedness* in teams that drive performance through excellence in their decision making.

Purpose

Purpose is a strong motivator. Kennedy's mission, announced in 1961, 'to achieving the goal, before this decade is out, of landing a man on the Moon and returning him safely to the Earth,' led to leaders, teams and many remarkable individuals working together to fulfil the destiny JFK had mapped out. Kennedy gave the people of the US, in particular those in NASA, a vision of the future. He gave them a powerful purpose, as brought home to us by the story of JFK and the NASA janitor. The story goes that when JFK was visiting NASA in

> Purpose is a strong motivator.

1962, he approached a janitor who was carrying a broom and asked what the man was doing. The man replied, 'Well, Mr President, I'm helping put a man on the moon.'[18]

Put simply, purpose inspires us. It motivates us to overcome obstacles, to work together to fulfil a common goal. Here are some aphorisms adopted by organisations in order to articulate their purpose and inspire others:

> General Electric — 'Building a world that works.'
> Samsung — 'Together for tomorrow.'
> Nestlé — 'Good food, Good life.'
> Fiat — 'Driven by passion.'
> Nike — 'Just do it.'
> National Australia Bank (NAB) — 'More than money.'
> Billabong — 'Life's better in boardshorts.'
> Canva — 'Design anything. Publish anywhere.'
> Vegemite — 'Tastes like Australia.'

Then there's Steve Jobs' famous 1980 mission statement for Apple: 'To make a contribution to the world by making tools for the mind that advance humankind.'[19]

Plenty of organisations have strong and clear statements of purpose, which does not mean all the teams in the organisation enjoy the same clarity. To be on the top rung of the team decision-making ladder, each team needs to understand how their role contributes to purpose. *Their* purpose. It does not stop there, of course. They also need clearly defined performance expectations and a clearly articulated strategy for how they will achieve their goals.

Talent

Talented teams have the right mix of skills, attitudes and creativity for the challenge ahead. Necessary skills are, of course, dependent on the challenge, while attitudes relate directly to the extent of the individual's alignment to the purpose of the team and the organisation. Creativity thrives in the right environment.

Once you have a team with the right skills, attitudes and creativity, their job is simply to identify the gaps between what they have achieved and what they need to achieve; to build bridges in the optimum priority order; and to get the traffic moving across them. The traffic could be data, it could be customers, it could be money. Whatever it is, it needs to flow across bridges built for the purpose. Metaphorically, a bridge not overly expensive, yet structurally sound. A bridge that looks nice enough rather than an architectural masterpiece.

> Once you have a team with the right skills, attitudes and creativity, their job is simply to identify the gaps between what they have achieved and what they need to achieve.

Sometimes, however, a new type of bridge needs to be built, one that requires higher levels of creativity and experimentation.

Why is experimentation so important? Experimentation is foundational to science, and scientists have a highly methodical approach to establishing facts. First, they establish a theory, then they design experiments to disprove the theory. If it can't be disproved, it becomes evidence-based and therefore accepted as legitimate. Just as no theory can ever be proved 100 per cent, in business we can never guarantee the success of a new product, but we can certainly increase our knowledge and hence our comfort levels by challenging its success through a few well-designed experiments.

Looking for a practical example and one that highlights the importance of an environment that supports creativity? Look no further than Ron Kohavi, Microsoft Distinguished Engineer and General Manager of the Analysis and Experimentation team at Microsoft's Applications and Services Group. Prior to joining Microsoft, he was Director of Data Mining and Personalisation at Amazon.com, Inc. where he found many examples of how experimentation can bring great rewards.

In a presentation entitled 'Practical Guide to Controlled Experiments on the Web: Listen to Your Customers not to the HiPPO', Kohavi describes a simple experiment run by Software Engineer Greg Linden of Amazon. Linden had the idea that as a customer shopped, other items could be recommended to them based on the items already in their cart. You may be familiar with the algorithm 'customers who bought this also bought . . .'

Linden proposed an experiment to establish whether the recommendation would cross-sell more items and increase the average sale size. Or would it instead distract customers from checking out and result in a loss of sales because it was all too hard? Enter what Kohavi refers to as the influence of the 'HiPPO (Highest Paid Person's Opinion)' The HiPPO had recommended stopping the project altogether, but because Amazon had created an environment that fostered creativity, Linden was allowed to run the experiment. It was hugely successful, and the rest is history.

With his teams at Microsoft, Kohavi has explored the value of experimentation over many years and has concluded that people think too short-term. Because they fear an experiment will fail there is cultural resistance. Kohavi has also worked out that '[o]ur intuition is poor, especially on novel ideas.' Enough said — creativity is where it's at.

Connectedness

As hybrid work took off in Covid times, there was talk of asynchronous vs synchronous teamwork, in particular for teams working across different time zones. Asynchronous teamwork referred to situations in which tasks instigated in one team's time zone would later be picked up by another team in another time zone. Synchronous teamwork referred to live collaboration facilitated by Zoom and MS Teams and other online collaboration support tools. I am using 'synchronous' differently, to refer to the way team members connect to find a flow to their decision making, irrespective of whether they are working across multiple time zones or working together online.

My definition of synchronous infers team members know and understand who is making a decision, and how and when it is being made. Further, they understand their role in supporting each decision as it is relevant to them, and they have worked out how to do so efficiently and effectively.

Synchronous teams deliver. They collaborate well and have the strongest buy-in for the outcomes produced. Because of this strong buy-in, combined with clarity of purpose and creative talent, they make compelling decisions. The team members feel a need to see them through.

> Synchronous teams deliver. They collaborate well and have the strongest buy-in for the outcomes produced.

As I pointed out in the decision value curve in figure 2, the thousands upon thousands of necessary implementation decisions are just as valuable as the big, strategic decisions. This means synchronous teams are an essential element for successful, agile delivery of planned outcomes.

The drivers of flow

I started the section headed 'How teams make decisions' by pointing out that teams make decisions by following a process. But here's the thing: often the 'process' is implicit rather than explicit, so each team member develops their own mental model of how decisions are made.

What is a mental model? It's how you and I form pictures in our minds to understand how the world works. As

James Clear explains in *Atomic Habits*, 'A mental model is an explanation of how something works. It is a concept, framework, or worldview that you carry around in your mind to help you interpret the world and understand the relationship between things. Mental models are deeply held beliefs about how the world works.'

Clearly, these models are personal and something each of us infers from our observations. And anything inferred is open to interpretation by us as individuals. Create a team of you, me and half a dozen others, and you have eight different versions. And as each of our versions interacts with the others, we create one of over 16 million possible variations of what each of us has observed. Is it any wonder teams are not always on the same page about the decisions being made!

For at least 30 years researchers have shown that moving beyond inferred mental models to shared mental models improves team performance. In 1991 Converse et al. published a paper distinguishing the more observable elements of good team performance, such as communication and feedback, from less observable elements, such as how a team coordinates activities and adapts them.[20] They explain that teams coordinate and adapt by anticipating the future needs and actions of team members and by predicting future levels of demand. To do so, team members 'draw from an invisible knowledge base' of how the team functions best. I cannot overemphasise how team connectedness, along with clarity of purpose and talent, are needed for this to work well.

In 2005 Jeffery et al. published a paper showing that team performance improves when the team collaborates to form a shared mental model.[21] In other words, the team co-creates the mental model. Again, the emphasis is on connectedness!

In a practical application of this field of research, Westli et al.[22] show that shared mental models are more important than classical teamwork skills for improving team performance in the medical management of trauma cases using a simulated trauma centre environment.

Now you've had the opportunity to think a little more about teams in your own organisation and how important they are in terms of effective decision making, I'm sure you can identify relevant areas of concern, such as a business case needing board approval. But I am equally sure you are recalling situations when teams were confused about how and why decisions were made, including bigger, strategic ones. And you are probably identifying the consequences, such as poor implementation of decisions made in the upper echelons of the organisation.

If your organisation has thought about this, you might already have in place strong governance frameworks or comprehensive decision-making guidelines for teams to follow regarding, for example, underwriting, sales forecasting, project approvals, and prioritisation and issuing grants from a fund. But in my experience, the norm is that for all that the guidelines help, inferred mental models of how decisions are actually made persist.

My work in recent years has convinced me that one or both of two critical elements are missing. These are *decision process maps* and *decision support tools* that go beyond guidelines (see figure 5). Together they make up a decision landscape that can be transmitted, or improved, to ensure decision flow, high-quality decisions and consistency of team decisions made at speed, creating higher and higher levels of performance.

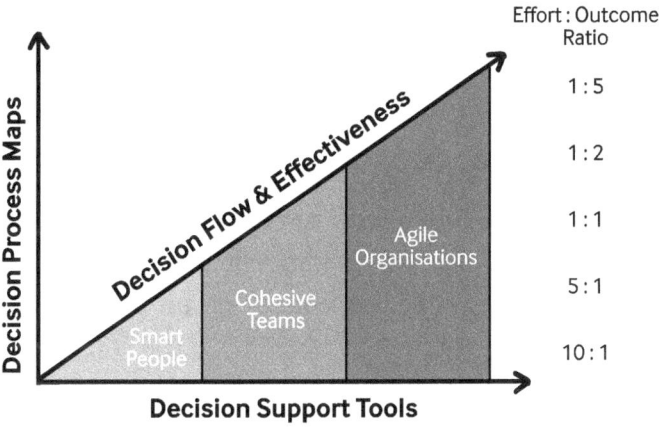

Figure 5: Decision landscapes

Why am I so sure that these two drivers, decision process maps and decision support tools, produce a decision flow that creates the agile organisation most leaders like you crave? Fair question. I'll answer that for you in the next chapter.

Chapter summary

The aim of decision making is to create value or protect it. Using the concept of a decision-value curve I explain a strategic decision has the same value as all the decisions made in implementing it. Which means, you need to focus on good decision making throughout your organisation or, as I call it, *decision flow* or simply *flow*.

Flow is about both quality of decision making and speed of decision making to create an agile organisation. The core elements required to create decision flow are smart people and cohesive teams.

Cohesive teams are clear on purpose, work creatively to achieve goals and communicate with a level of synchronicity that ensures good communication for decision making. The results are compelling decisions the team will support with verve.

The drivers of flow that create the synchronicity needed are decision process maps and decision support tools. The process maps get the team on the same page about how the best decisions need to be made or escalated, and they can be used to identify where decision support tools are needed to improve consistency for recurring decisions or for ensuring good processes are followed at key times for one-off bigger decisions.

Part 2

Faster, better decision making

3

Creating flow

In the absence of an explicit mental model for making decisions in particular contexts, you and I have acknowledged that team members will establish an inferred mental model that blocks flow. It leads instead to inconsistencies, errors and the necessity for rework. While some decisions follow formal processes, others do not. And even when formal processes exist, team decision making is affected by individual and team bias as well as by the causes of what Kahneman et al. term *noise*. Let's now consider the role of decision process maps and decision support tools in counteracting bias and noise and driving decision flow to maximise team performance at every level of the organisation. Then we will focus in on the making of more strategic decisions.

> While some decisions follow formal processes, others do not.

The first time I truly appreciated the value of these two

drivers was when I was approached by a government agency that had a critical role in protecting the natural environment. They were seeking to provide clarity and visibility on key points for some of their decision-making processes. These included the frequency of decision making, the people and processes that support those decisions, and the flows of knowledge that are required to inform or report on them. They were also seeking my recommendations on decision support tools that could be developed to assist in improving the flow of decisions.

In this situation, my knowledge of decision making within the complexity of organisations overlapped with my knowledge of how the chemical and process industries manage complexity in operations. I had a clear understanding of the power of combining decision process maps with decision support tools. Let me explain.

When designing a chemical or other process plant, designers map out the process using what are called Piping and Instrument Diagrams or P&IDs. These diagrams use well-established nomenclature for a tank, a pump, a catalytic cracker (used in oil refineries), an indicator of level or of pressure in a tank, and so on. And because of my experience in the identification and management of risk in chemical plants, I was fully aware of the benefits of mapping these processes in more detail *when necessary*, both to support understanding of the process and to minimise the risk of missing anything critical either during design or should modifications to the process be required. Some of the industry's worst disasters have resulted from seemingly minor process modifications. In a chemical plant near the village of Flixborough in the UK in 1974, the temporary replacement of a flange connecting a pipe to a vessel caused an explosion that killed or seriously injured half of the 72 people on site.[23]

Mapping is one thing. However, with something as complicated as a chemical processing plant, the use of a critical decision support tool called HAZOP proved essential for the industry. HAZOP stands for 'hazard and operability'. The process is used line by line, vessel by vessel, through an entire P&ID to identify challenges to a plant's operation. It is essential to the process from the design stage to avoid faults during pilot or operation and is called upon when a change is being made to make sure a hazardous or inoperable situation is not created inadvertently, as happened in the Flixborough disaster.

Armed with this understanding, when I began my work with the government agency, I developed decision process maps with each of the seven different teams involved. As you'll appreciate, any agency working to protect the environment is operating in an extremely complex domain. Some teams had already mapped their processes. Nonetheless, with the benefit of my knowledge of the importance of detailed process maps in the chemical industry, I was able to improve their existing maps by identifying missing details

> Any agency working to protect the environment is operating in an extremely complex domain.

and helping them see their importance. I compiled maps that allowed team members to *see* the process they had been following to make decisions that were otherwise *inferred*. For example, a critical decision process that used a rule of thumb for quick estimation of the impact of an incident involved just one person and had never been documented!

I had experience in developing decision support tools of all kinds through my roles as both a chemical engineer and a management consultant for a range of other government agencies and private sector companies. I was able to bring all this history to bear on the decision process maps for the government agency so they could identify which type of decision support tool would provide most benefit at each high-priority decision point.

For example, I had introduced decision trees to assist a government agency to determine whether or not to stand as head contractor with a private sector company or as subcontractor for important overseas development initiatives. I also used decision trees when working with a private sector company that needed to choose between two options for the location for their new head office. (I know, I know but the CEO wanted the hip-and-happening office and the logistics were a nightmare. They needed the decision trees I helped them build to 'assist' the CEO to choose the achievable option!)

I also assisted an emergency services government agency to build a rapid risk-ranking tool for a particular type of operation that involved shredding the current approach that was packed with, and wrapped in, red tape. I was able to help them reduce decision times for some operations from hours to minutes — critical, of course, for emergency services.

I have also assisted in the design of multi-criteria decision analysis tools for multiple clients to help them conduct strategic options assessments of various kinds, and have assisted numerous clients with decision support tools to help them determine whether various options were within or outside the risk appetite defined and set by the board.

To return to the government agency involved in protecting the natural environment, for some of the teams the mapping of the processes was the most important step because it helped them to identify bottlenecks. We worked on decision support tools that would speed up the decision process by authorising staff to use the tools to make decisions without referring to a higher authority.

For other teams the value lay in identifying what was driving perceived inconsistencies in decision making by stakeholders. For example, why was a party given a permit or funding in one instance but not in another instance when the circumstances seemed very similar to applicants familiar with the requirements? Such decisions might be the effect of unclear guidelines or inconsistency of information sources, or the failure to assess and weigh different criteria against each other — for example, economic vs environmental impact.

Since being part of that project, I have helped many organisations to implement decision support tools using the decision process to, for example, operationalise their risk appetite framework. Used as a decision support tool, such a framework can ensure decisions are made faster because those involved know they are operating within an agreed appetite for risk taking. The highlight for me was when I worked with a Canadian government agency. The agency had been given very strong instructions to be less risk averse, which required a considerable shift in mindset, given the staff's previous experience of what happens when things go wrong!

Another standout example of the benefits of mapping decision landscapes and designing decision support for staff is that of a government agency I assisted to map the decision landscape for the design of a product traceability system. From product source through processing and all the way to the end customer, they used the latest in tracking and tracing technology — all with a compliance program to oversee the industry. The system had to take into account a large number of stakeholders with different tasks, different information needs and conflicting regulatory constraints. By identifying the most critical points in the process I was able to help the team

> From product source through processing and all the way to the end customer, they used the latest in tracking and tracing technology — all with a compliance program to oversee the industry.

gain clarity on their starting point for design and to picture an end point for optimal design of the system.

To bring this all together for you, let me explain the three key areas of focus for creating flow — faster, better decision making delivering more consistency for stakeholders affected by the decisions made. As figure 6 illustrates, flow facilitates recurring decisions by focusing first on *criticality* of decisions; second on the *design* of the decision landscape; and third on the *veracity* of the decision support tools created to support decision making.

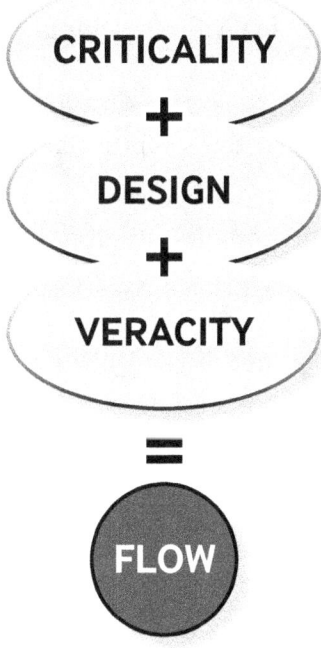

Figure 6: Creating flow

In the next three chapters I will delve into each of these. My aim is to give you enough understanding to enable you to develop your own methodology, should you wish to do so. A bit of trial and error will be ahead of you, but the benefits will be your reward.

Chapter summary

My years of researching decision making, along with my experience as a chemical engineer of mapping complex chemical manufacturing processes as diagrams on a page, through to my work with clients developing decision support tools, have led me to understand the key three things you need to focus on to create flow in your organisation:

1. a method to *categorise* decisions so they can be handled differently as appropriate
2. being diligent in the *design* of your optimum decision landscape to promote and support flow
3. ensuring the *veracity* of your decision support tools.

Each is explained in the following chapters.

4

Categorically critical

It all starts with the criticality of the overall decision landscape and the decisions to be made within it. Some decisions are potentially life-changing, some are more mundane and others exist along the continuum. You don't take the same approach to making every decision. You don't seek the opinions of others for every decision. You don't do a whole lot of thinking or analysis for every decision. But sometimes you do.

> Some great thinkers, both academics and business folk alike, have put their mind to categorising decisions.

Some great thinkers, both academics and business folk alike, have put their mind to categorising decisions. Let me take you through some of the thinking around this.

Kahneman

In his bestselling book *Thinking, Fast and Slow*, Daniel Kahneman explained that we all use two decision-making systems. System One is fast thinking and uses rules of thumb or your instincts or gut feel. System Two is much slower and requires logical thinking. We automatically categorise decisions according to either System One or System Two thinking.

If we apply this categorisation process correctly, we assign to System One the kinds of decisions we make often, or those for which the consequence of getting it wrong are not super critical, such as choosing a restaurant for dinner. We assign more significant decisions to System Two.

Kahneman explains how we often get this categorisation wrong. We use fast thinking when we should use slow thinking. This is because we are quick to jump to conclusions. We don't stop to do the maths, or ask ourselves if this is all it seems.

Bezos and Branson

Richard Branson and Jeff Bezos have a similar take on categorising decisions. Branson, founder of businesses as diverse as Virgin Records and Virgin Airlines, talks about decisions that are a one-way door and those that are two-way doors.[24] You can come back through a two-way door; if you choose a one-way door, you can't reverse the decision.

Bezos, founder of online retailer Amazon and one of the

world's wealthiest people, introduced to Amazon the concept of Type 1 and Type 2 decisions. He is very comfortable with his team making Type 2 decisions straight out because they are reversible.[25] In fact, he insists they follow this system.

Type 1 decisions, on the other hand, he defines as 'consequential and irreversible or nearly irreversible'.[26] That is, they will be very damaging if we don't get them right. Type 1 decisions need to be very well considered. Type 2 decisions can be made much faster.

The message from these icons of industry is don't confuse the two types of decision making, since to do so may lead, on the one hand, to a slowing of the organisation or, on the other, to adverse consequences for the organisation and its stakeholders.

McKinsey – De Smet, Lackey and Weiss

Leading management consulting firm McKinsey has developed a four-category model to aid decision makers.[27] They refer to high-impact decisions as either 'big-bet' or 'cross-cutting', depending on the degree of understanding of the decision being made, and lower-impact decisions as 'ad hoc' or 'delegated', again depending on the degree of understanding of the decision being made.

This terminology is one of the best aspects of this model because of the picture it paints in one's mind. A big-bet is a big-bet, no two ways about it. It implies a one-way door and a highly consequential decision. Cross-cutting emphasises the scale of the impact of a decision and the need to consider a broad set of stakeholders to optimise it. The terminology of the lower-impact categories makes it clear that some are ad hoc, routine, while others are among the plethora of decisions that pop up every day and can be delegated.

Snowden

David Snowden, a management consultant and team leader, developed the Cynefin Framework for decision making. I find it helpful to think of it as the 4-Cs of decision categorisation — Core, Complicated, Complex and Chaotic.

The Cynefin Framework offers guidance on how to make decisions in each of these categories:

- *Core.* These decisions require initial sensing — that is, identification of the key attributes of the decision, which will then be placed into a more rigid framework to enable the decision to be made. An example is basic budgeting decisions on which inflation or interest rates to utilise.
- *Complicated.* Again, initial sensing is followed by analysis. Here the broader governance framework of your organisation comes into play in order to decide, for example, which supplier to contract to build a high-value piece of equipment. While not quite like the commissioning of a chemical plant with the irrefutable laws of physics and chemistry in play once it is commissioned, it is still a relatively complicated decision that will require the assistance

of experienced legal advisers and contract managers to navigate the usual areas of risk.

- *Complex.* Here the framework starts in a different space. Complex decisions require some probing before you move to sensemaking. To expand our school-of-fish analogy to a complex system, we might think about the effect of the presence of a predator and how it affected the school's movement. Some experimentation will be required and particular rules will need to be followed to maximise efficacy and minimise the likelihood of adverse impact. An example of a complex decision would be opening a business in a foreign country where laws, regulations and cultural norms are different. You would be well advised to do some probing before making the big-bet investment.

- *Chaos.* As a result of the Covid pandemic, all decision makers experienced a degree of chaos. Here the framework calls for action first, sensemaking second, followed by the next set of actions. In this situation almost anything goes. However, I do advise you do a reality check with your values to make sure you, and they, remain aligned.

> As a result of the Covid pandemic, all decision makers experienced a degree of chaos.

Whitefield

I guess you know who I am referring to here. Yes, yours truly. I regularly look through a risk lens — as, I have no doubt, do all those I've just referred to. However, I am more explicit about how decisions should be made.

Figure 7 shows a combination of the Bezos categorisation of Type 1 and 2 decisions, the McKinsey model and the Cynefin Framework. The decisions on the top row, Type 1A and Type 2A, are based on what might be considered sufficient information to make a decision. The level of information required might be higher for some than others, although Bezos suggests 70 per cent is the cut-off.[28] For decisions on the bottom row, Type 1B and Type 2B, decision makers have less information to work with, which means potential outcomes are more uncertain.

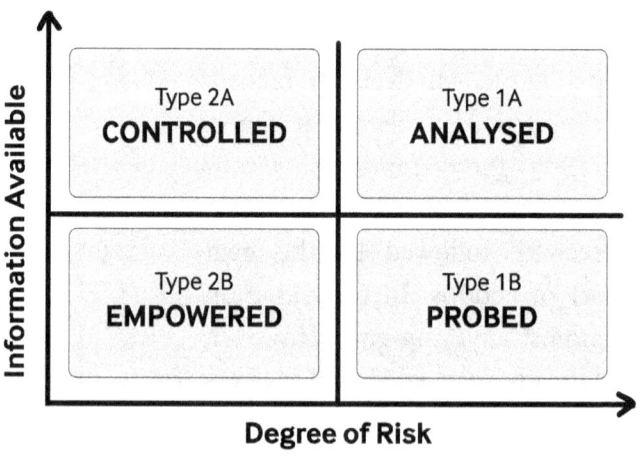

Figure 7: Decision categorisation matrix

Now consider risk. Because of a lack of information, Type 1B decisions (consequential and likely irreversible) require careful consideration of the risks being taken — that is to say, they require a degree of formal risk assessment. Type 2B decisions (reversible or at least less consequential) do not. And this is where I have adapted some of the terminology or language of the McKinsey model and the Cynefin Framework. Because a lot is known about them, Type 2A decisions should be able to be kept under good control. The risks are well understood, which allows for the design of controls that will help ensure optimal decisions. The better the design of the controls, the faster the decision making. For Type 2B decisions, for which levels of information and hence knowledge are low, decision makers should be empowered through delegated authorities or decision rights. You will rely on the experience and judgement of delegates to get the vast majority of these decisions right.

Finally, this model suggests that higher-risk decisions that require high levels of information — that is, Type 1A — should be analysed and actions taken following the Cynefin Framework's guidance for Complicated decisions. Those Type 1s that don't meet the bar for sufficient information — Type 1B — are treated as Complex using the Cynefin model: the situation should be probed, taking on bite-size chunks until you have learned more and are ready to place the big-bet.

Now you have a model for categorising decisions, let's add in another component of criticality — time.

Time critical

For flow to happen, decisions must be made as fast as practicably possible. Categorisation doesn't determine the time you take to make a decision; that depends on other factors. Setting aside emergency decision making, Type 1 decisions, irreversible and consequential, demand a thorough process to maximise the probability that the optimum decision will be made. However, the processes will be different for one-off strategic decisions and for recurring decisions. For example, compare a first-time acquisition with an organisation that has a strategy of acquiring small businesses in order to become the dominant player. The latter can develop a playbook for the acquisition team to follow to speed decision making. As is the case for Type 1 decisions, Type 2 decisions require an appropriate process that minimises red tape to promote speed while combatting bias and Kahneman et al.'s noise.

> For flow to happen, decisions must be made as fast as practicably possible.

Once you have determined how you will categorise the decisions your organisation makes, you will need to map your decision landscape to clarify just how different kinds of decisions are made. Categorisation and mapping will allow you to see whether some are being made using inappropriate processes. You may identify processes that suffer from bottlenecks or decisions that have a history of being sub-optimal, either of which could point to bias or noise. Once your landscape is mapped and you have identified trouble spots, you can design decision-appropriate support tools.

Chapter summary

To create decision flow, you need to categorise decisions so they can be handled appropriately. Business gurus like Bezos and Branson have their methods, as does consulting powerhouse McKinsey and complexity guru David Snowden. I introduce my four categories:

- *Empowered.* Staff are able to make decisions quickly, for themselves, and move on.
- *Controlled.* Staff are able to make decisions following clearly defined guidelines or more rigid controls.
- *Probed.* Information is uncertain and we need to dig further as time allows.
- *Analysed.* Decisions of higher risk with plenty of information to consider.

5

Delicate design

Years ago I became involved with a major defence assurance program. I was engaged for a princely sum and embarked on delivering the project as agreed. When I delivered my first major milestone, the officer in charge said, 'Thanks, but that's not particularly interesting, is it?' I agreed. Then the insightful officer said, 'So what is the question you should be asking me?' I instantly replied, 'What are the key risks the program is aiming to assure?' From that moment the project shifted and as a result I delivered a much more valuable and insightful piece of work.

I start this chapter with this reflection because it emphasises one important check you need to make before spending a significant amount of your precious resources on mapping your decision landscape. You need to ask yourself, 'Is the team being asked the right question?' If the answer is 'Yes', you can proceed. If it's 'No' or 'Perhaps not', you need to resolve this first.

For example, you may ask a team to work on improving a product's design and ask them to map how decisions will be made on each design alteration. However, instead of asking how to improve the design of a product, perhaps you should be asking the team 'How do we replace this product with something better?'

> Instead of asking how to improve the design of a product, perhaps you should be asking the team 'How do we replace this product with something better?'

I have mentioned Jeffery et al.'s research that showed the co-creation of a mental model of team decision making aimed at improving performance. A focus of their research was the benefits to teams of co-creating mental models for new situations. For example, if an executive team has never acquired another organisation as a team, they will benefit from developing a model to follow to make a successful acquisition.

They observed that in the absence of a co-created model, the previously inferred mental model that has worked for some time can lead to groupthink. The team becomes complacent and relies on existing processes and norms, and holds back on airing their thoughts on a decision. They conclude that a critical skill set for any team is its ability to co-create mental models and they put forward five 'imperatives' for doing so effectively:

- *Imperative 1.* Clarification of team objectives and tasks, environment and variables

- *Imperative 2.* Establishing roles and responsibilities
- *Imperative 3.* Information processing, communication, and collaborative modelling rules and procedures
- *Imperative 4.* Knowledge of team members' background and style
- *Imperative 5.* Collaborative modelling scheme.

When I train teams in co-creation of mental models, I explain that the prime objective of a delicate design is to bring clarity and visibility to decision processes. I then introduce my three-step process for mapping mental models that achieve these imperatives and more. They are Collaboration, Collation and Clarification (see figure 8).

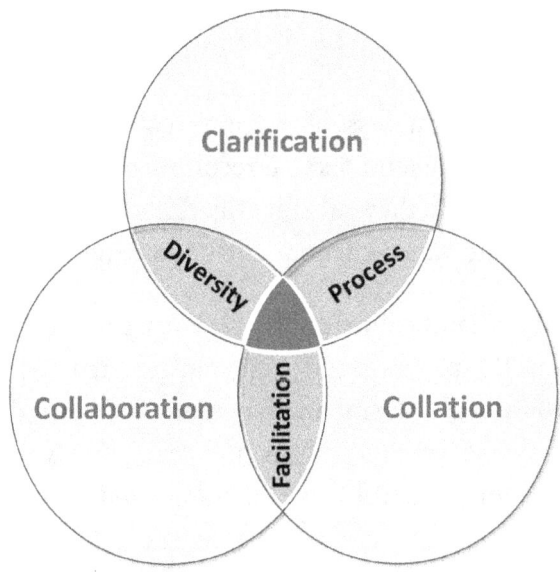

Figure 8: Mental model mapping process

This process applies whether you are mapping an existing decision process to improve it or developing a process map for a type of decision not previously made — for example, your organisation's first acquisition of a competitor, or a shift from product or process improvement to replacement.

Collaboration

Jeffery et al.'s Imperative 5 refers to a scheme that can be a process map, a cause-and-effect diagram or any other technique to create a blueprint for how people think, decide and act. My go-to scheme is a decision process map using agreed nomenclature for the various symbols used. While collaboration in the development of the scheme, usually a decision process map, is essential, collaboration starts way earlier.

Maximising the success of a team's collaborative design all starts with stakeholders. I recommend a stakeholder analysis in which they are identified and their roles and impacts (explicit and potential) are documented.

Next is the identification of the team that will collaborate to develop the process map. You want diversity in design, just as you want diversity on teams for good team decision making. While you may think the team that will utilise the process map should first collaborate and co-create it, I recommend you invite key stakeholders to be part of the team from the outset. Each will offer unique insights into the decision-making challenge, in particular staff needing to feed information into the process in a timely manner.

Not every team member or stakeholder needs to be involved at every stage of the development of the decision landscape; some will avoid taking part, for example, due to time restraints. You would be wise to use your powers of influence and persuasion (the subject of my book *Persuasive Advising: How to Turn Red Tape into Blue Ribbon*) to make sure they become willing participants. Then you will be ready to move on to Collation, the next step in the process.

> Not every team member or stakeholder needs to be involved at every stage of the development of the decision landscape

Collation

In the development of a schematic diagram of a chemical processing plant, the core elements required for the design are known. For example, the designer will know that in a given section of the process there will be a distillation column, a reactor or some other piece of equipment. Each one of these will have a number of long-established critical components associated with them — pipes, pumps or heat exchangers, for example. And each piece of equipment will have a set of key controls that monitor the process and make adjustments to manage fluctuations and keep the process operating within design specifications. Knowing these things makes the job of the designer of the schematic much, much easier.

What the designer has is a collation of elements of the schematic they know will need to be included. You will also need to collate a list of what needs to be incorporated in your process map. A typical list of items I give a team I am working with to collate is:

- *Objectives* — decision(s) and objective(s)
- *Inputs* — into the decision process, including initiating actions and data
- *Variables* — that may impact decision outcomes; these may include the inputs to decisions and the pros and cons of a decision, for example when balancing the needs of stakeholders as identified in the stakeholder analysis
- *Tasks* — including, for example, research, consultation, communication and recording
- *Rights* — roles and responsibilities, including decision rights
- *Determinants* — rules, regulations, policies and procedures that guide or determine decisions.

Next the team start building the process map. That is, they take the information collected and get it down on 'paper', which in the world of online collaboration usually involves using a tool like Mural (my preference), Microsoft Whiteboard or similar, all of which are excellent for designing decision landscapes. These tools allow a large amount of data to be collated on a single page (called a mural in Mural), with ease of navigation and the ability to zoom in and out to see the detail and the big picture as required.

Mural also has a broad set of shapes and icons you can use to establish your symbol nomenclature. Figure 9 is an example of a process map for a government team that issues permits. It includes a key showing a typical set of symbols that will suffice for most business processes, though many more options are available within Mural.

My advice is to collate more, rather than less, early in the process. It is easier to cut things out than to backtrack because something important was forgotten. A word of warning: some involved in the co-creation are likely to 'hate' the detail. Hold your ground as best you can and deliver a decision landscape map appropriately scaled back when the time comes.

> My advice is to collate more, rather than less, early in the process. It is easier to cut things out than to backtrack because something important was forgotten.

Having a process for collation of a decision map is only part of the secret to a great outcome. The other is facilitation of the process. Although you may have assembled a great team with broad diversity of insights, as you know, and will keep discovering, getting the best from this team is not straightforward. This is where a deliberate approach to facilitating the collation process is required.

68 | TEAM THINK

5: DELICATE DESIGN | 69

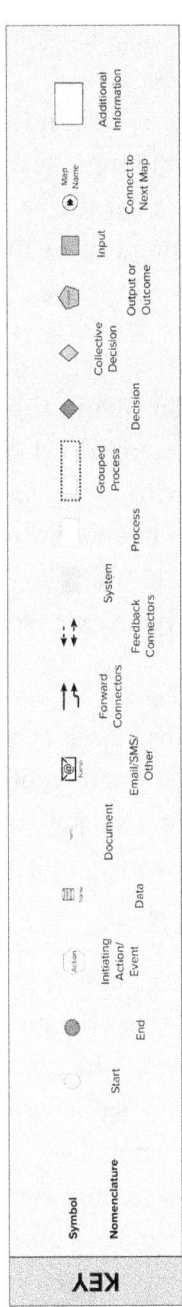

Figure 9: Sample decision process map

> Having a process for collation of a decision map is only part of the secret to a great outcome. The other is facilitation of the process.

I am a very experienced and, I like to think, a very good facilitator based on the feedback and success I have had facilitating for clients. However, I am frequently reminded that if you don't prepare adequately for facilitating a team session, it is highly likely problems will arise. At the very least you won't achieve as much as you wanted to in the time allowed — and someone, if not everyone in the team, is likely to notice!

> I am frequently reminded that if you don't prepare adequately for facilitating a team session, it is highly likely problems will arise.

My most recent reminder at the time of writing this book occurred when I became impatient with someone who soon went into the equivalent of a workshop intensive care ward as a patient. Let me explain what happened.

First, the proximate cause of my impatience. She was providing lots of detail I was not looking for and would talk over others I was trying to listen to. Before long I found myself interrupting her to redirect the conversation.

Why was she providing so much detail? Either because she was feeling threatened or because she felt I was operating on her turf, or both. At the end of the workshop, she asked me the purpose of the workshop, which I had explained in a pre-meeting and at the beginning of the workshop. Despite my impatience I forced myself to listen and began to detect her previously unspoken concerns, managing to recover some trust. I built on that, and the project ran smoothly from there.

I had made several mistakes. First, I had not checked that she clearly understood the purpose of the workshop. That is, I had not asked her to 'say it back to me in her words'. Second, I had failed to properly identify the potential for me to be a threat, given her role and what she had already said at the pre-meeting. And third, I had not made an effort to build on her accomplishments and emphasise how my role aimed to enhance the significance of her work.

I'm no rookie, but these were rookie errors.

The secret to great facilitation of a process decision mapping exercise is preparation. Consider the stakeholders in the room and their 'agendas'. Consider the number of people involved, how it is to be run and the process you will follow, and develop a plan for the time allowed. At the start of the session, confirm the purpose, the objectives set for the time allowed and the process you will follow. And let everyone know how you are going to go about pushing the team forward when things get bogged down so they are prepared for it and won't be offended.

When it comes to facilitation, the old saying 'A little preparation goes a long way' can't be overemphasised. You will avoid difficult conversations and perhaps alienating difficult individuals.

Clarification

In this next step, a full complement of the process map design team is required to clarify the decision landscape. Some good old-fashioned 'appreciative enquiry' will lead to a much clearer picture of the current process to be mapped, or will lead to a better design of a new process.

For an existing process, the team will need to review the decision landscape and assess the quality and consistency of each decision point. This is also an opportunity to question elements of the process as there may be bottlenecks that can be reduced or even eliminated with some redesign. For many processes there will be existing guidance documentation and decision support tools such as templates and decision trees. These all need to be critiqued.

If a team is building a process map for a new decision — for example, a decision landscape for acquisitions — the team will need to identify existing decision support tools and templates that may be utilised in the process; for example, an existing business-case template. Any tool identified needs to be assessed for its veracity to support good decision making — that is, the extent to which it can be relied on to provide sound, consistent outcomes. More on assessing such tools in the following chapter.

Finalising the decision landscape may require multiple iterations, particularly when you are documenting an existing process for which an inferred mental model has been created. Team members will have a picture of the landscape in their heads, and everyone's picture will be slightly different.

If you follow this process, you will achieve the prime objective of a delicate design I mentioned earlier to provide clarity and visibility of decision-making processes.

Chapter summary

The secret to the design of decision process maps is the three Cs: Collation, Collaboration and Clarification. Research shows that in the absence of an agreed map, team members develop their own mental models of the decision process and seldom are two people's models the same.

I suggest you involve the whole team in the development of the map. I have laid out the process for developing process maps and I encourage you to facilitate a robust discussion on how you can improve the decision process and the points in the process at which a decision support tool would be of benefit.

> The secret to the design of decision process maps is the three Cs: Collation, Collaboration and Clarification.

6

Vibrant veracity

Now to the last step in the process for creating flow in your organisation to maximise team performance. You need to establish the veracity of any existing decision support tools and design new tools where none exist for decisions that are noisy or generally sub-optimal. Some decision support tools tackle group or individual bias and noise, while others turn a decision from the gut feel of a gambler to considered risk taking, and still others simply speed up decision making by guiding decision makers so they are able to act quickly.

> There are many types of decision support tools, and bespoke tools can be designed for unique circumstances.

There are many types of decision support tools, and bespoke tools can be designed for unique circumstances. The next section outlines the set of decision support tools I most commonly work with. I provide a brief explanation of each one, their general application, and some of the pros and cons of their use.

Decision trees

Decision trees are good tools to aid decision makers when considering decision criteria that can be assessed based on a small number of alternatives (for example, Yes/No or High/Medium/Low). Two examples are illustrated below. In the first (figure 10), a decision tree has been created to guide a team leader on what action to take in response to an incident report, in which A, B and C are all possible compliance actions. In this case the team leader needs to consider five questions — priority rating, reliability of source, strength of evidence, seriousness of offence and level of intent — by answering either Y/N or H/M/L to determine the action to take.

In the second example (figure 11), a decision maker is asked to consider four questions on how best to deal with a specific risk identified in a project through allocation of the risk within a contract. In this example, one outcome may be straightforward, such as paying to insure the risk, while another may require negotiation or further analysis. The point is, decision support tools can be utilised anywhere along a process, not just to determine final outcomes.

Decision trees, like decision maps, work best when they are co-designed by the team to gain agreement on the flow of reasoning and the recommended endpoints. Each decision point on the tree should be accompanied by explanatory guidelines to help reduce bias and noise.

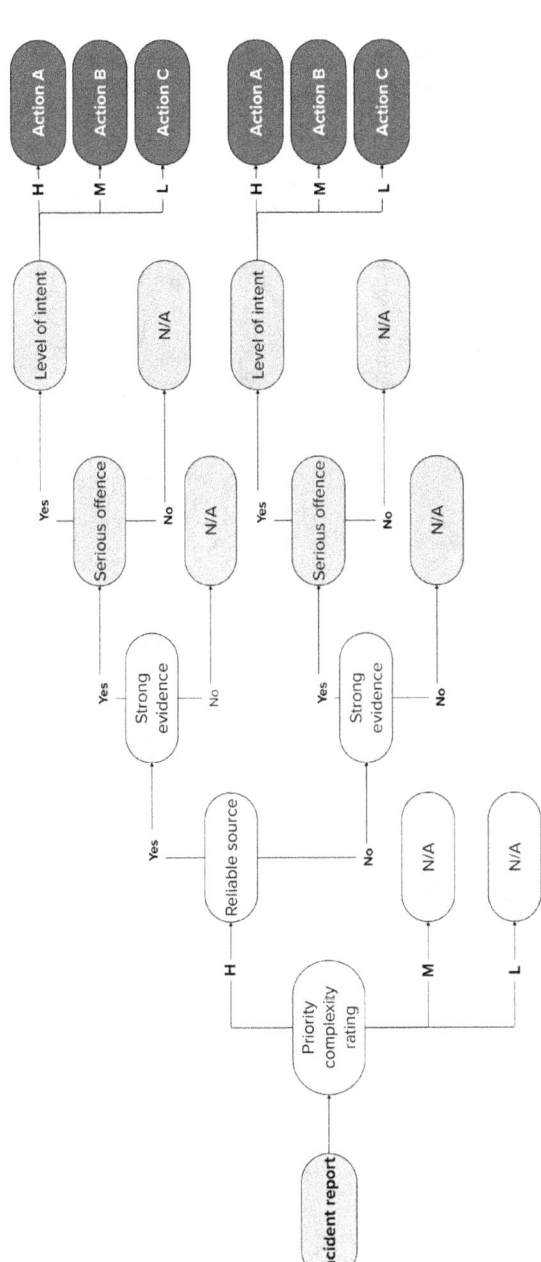

Figure 10: Sample decision tree for incident response

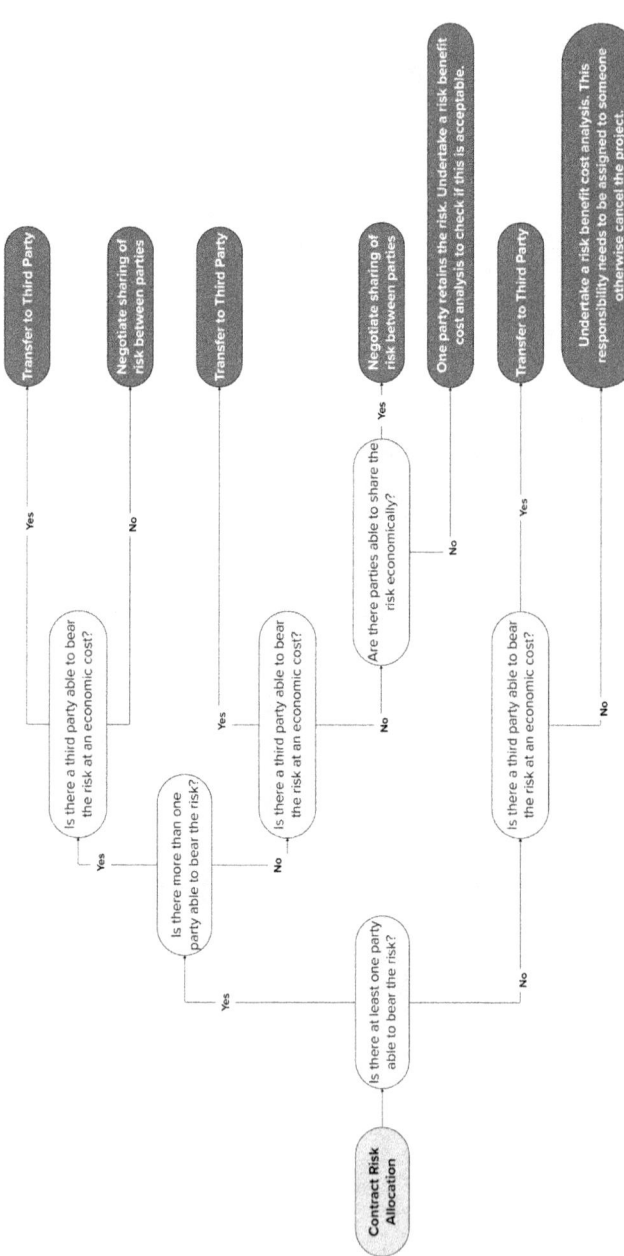

Figure 11: Sample decision tree for allocating risk in a contract

Multi-criteria decision analysis (MCDA)

MCDAs aid decision makers in weighing up a diverse set of criteria. Consider the examples below:

Values Impact Assessment of a Permit Application					
Weighting	20%	25%	25%	30%	100%
Impacting Activity	Biodiversity	Ecology	Community	Economy	Total
Recreational Fishing	-35	-15	15	55	9.50
Floating Dock	0	15	50	10	19.25
Use of Large Marine Craft	-15	-15	10	15	0.25
					29.00

Figure 12: Sample MCDA for permit application

Comparing Suppliers				
Weighting	50%	20%	30%	100%
Impacting Activity	Location	Size	Value for Money	Total
Supplier One	2	4	2	2.4
Supplier Two	2	3	3	3.0
Supplier Three	4	1	3	3.1

Figure 13: Sample MCDA for supplier selection

Figure 12 illustrates assisting a decision maker in balancing economic benefits and community impacts with environmental impacts. In this example, three activities requesting a permit need to be rated against four criteria.

In this case, a positive 29 is scored. The assessment MCDA would have guidelines as to whether this number could lead to approval or not, given some large negative scores for biodiversity.

Figure 13 is an example of where this type of tool could be used in the private sector to assess which supplier to contract with based on location, size and value for money. Each is scored out of 5, where 5 is best. The guidelines for this tool would need to address the possibility of total scores being close to each other — in this case, a 3 and a 3.1. The guideline may suggest considering if any one factor was significantly negative for one of the suppliers — in this case, a score of 1 on size for Supplier Three. This may be enough to guide the decision maker to Supplier Two.

This type of tool is helpful in reducing bias and noise, as it requires a decision maker to focus on rating each weighted criterion independently of other considerations.

The difficulty of developing an MCDA tool is in gaining agreement on weightings and how they are combined to determine a decision outcome that allows users to feel confident that it provides a 'fair' assessment. A result will sometimes seem counterintuitive to the decision maker and may lead to revisiting the application of a weighting, which may introduce bias and noise into the decision process.

Consequently, clear guidelines for rating criteria are required and will be the result of multiple rounds of testing and refining the tool against past decisions, as well as during initial implementation. The accuracy of the tool will be monitored over an extensive period by recording decisions based on the tool and compared against the known or assessed outcomes of each decision.

Once in use, mechanisms will be put into place to hold decision makers accountable for how appropriately they applied the guidelines.

Risk assessment

Risk assessment is a valuable technique to assess whether a risk is worth taking or to compare the risk of one option against others. It can be very beneficial for Type 2 decisions by creating a standard form of assessment, such as a risk-scoring tool that allows a decision maker to quickly rate risk based on the combined experience of those designing the tool.

> Risk assessment is a valuable technique to assess whether a risk is worth taking or to compare the risk of one option against others.

Figure 14 shows an example of a basic risk scoring tool. The tool is used to rate three elements of physical security risk between 1 and 5. Each one is weighted to give a risk score, and these are added together to determine the overall risk rating. The total score (in this case 330) determines whether the risk is low, medium, high or extreme by the settings within the tool agreed by experts at the design stage.

This type of tool has similar advantages and disadvantages to a multi-criteria decision analysis tool in that it ensures user confidence. Significant thought must go into determining the criteria, their weightings (if any), the guidelines for scoring them and the risk levels the scoring produces.

The design of risk assessment tools should be as simple as practicable, given the complexity and importance of the assessment. This will:

- facilitate consideration of the commonly understood areas of risk
- encourage identification of unusual areas of risk
- require documentation of the reasons for the assessed risk level.

No.	Element Being Assessed	Rating (1 low, 5 ext.)	Weighting	Risk Score
	Capability			
1	Physical ability to inflict harm	2	10	20
2	Weapons – availability of firearms or other weapons	4	40	160
				Total = 180
	Intent			
1	Propensity for violence	3	50	150
				Total = 150
			Combined Total = 330	High

Figure 14: Sample risk scoring tool

Risk appetite

Clarification of the organisation's appetite for risk taking facilitates speed and consistency of decision making.

Risk appetite and associated tolerances can be straightforward or they can be complex and difficult to measure. For example, a sales director could set a straightforward risk threshold on the number of new leads generated per quarter. Based on experience, once the number drops below that threshold, sales targets in the following quarter are not met.

It is more difficult to articulate a risk threshold for innovative marketing of products. While it is easy to say the sales director has a high tolerance for innovative advertising campaigns, it is not altogether clear what is meant by that and many advertisers have found themselves missing the mark with their target audience and killing sales. A recent example is the Woolworths ANZAC Day advertising campaign. ANZAC Day is Australia and New Zealand's most significant veterans day. The campaign encouraged consumers to upload images of war veterans to social media, which were then transformed into a commemorative picture with the Woolworths logo and the tagline 'Fresh In Our Memories'. The campaign aimed to commemorate ANZAC Day and connect with consumers through a tribute to veterans.

The campaign faced swift and ferocious backlash for trivialising the use of the word ANZAC and commercialising a day of national significance. And for not seeking endorsement of veterans bodies such as the RSL (Returned Services League).

However, if guidance on appetite for risk is not provided, it will be open to interpretation by decision makers, which can vary greatly based on personal perspective. Hence, any risk-appetite tool developed should be reviewed to ensure it provides sufficient guidance to reduce subjectivity in evaluating risk levels, preferably via measurable tolerances.

An example of a simple but effective risk appetite decision support tool is to place programs and projects of work into one of four categories, such as Averse, Cautious, Accepting or Open. Guidance is provided to program or project leaders on what is expected of them in terms of the extent of controls they must put in place based on which category they are operating in. For example, a project in the Averse column might be required to have independent assurance reviews to ensure it is on track and operating within parameters. Projects in the Accepting category may be able to accept and carry certain kinds of high risk because the benefits are deemed to outweigh any drawbacks.

Anonymous voting

In some cases, team decisions are best made by the team rather than the team leader — for example, when representatives of multiple departments need to agree on a course of action. As I have discussed, group decisions can be flawed in numerous ways, the effects of peer pressure and

6: VIBRANT VERACITY | 85

of the loudest voice in the room being just two common problems. Anonymous voting helps to combat these.

It's also perfectly acceptable for a team, including an executive team, to determine a course of action based on anonymous voting, especially when the best path forward is highly uncertain and no one person has sufficient expertise to make the call.

Research has shown that taking the average for the group is highly likely to be more accurate than any one individual's 'guess'.[29] Other research shows that decisions can be further improved by groups creating a robust average of assessments from which extreme outliers are excluded.[30]

Implementing an anonymous voting tool can be relatively straightforward, depending on what is being assessed. A straightforward example is providing a range of choices across an interval scale where the intervals are proportionate (say, $10m, $20m, $30m to $100m), and the scores are averaged for the number of voters. The same can't be said for an ordinal scale. And there are differences between a practical and an academic or pure statistical view when it comes to averaging one type of ordinal scale to another.

> Implementing an anonymous voting tool can be relatively straightforward, depending on what is being assessed.

One example is an ordinal scale that rates degrees of pain out of 10, where a 6 is worse than a 3. This would not imply that a 6 is double the pain of a 3; it's just higher, but not as high as a 7. Averaging is not such a good idea here as the scale may not be perceived as having equal intervals.

Another example is a Likert scale rating a statement like 'The product will be a good cultural fit with our existing processes' from *Strongly agree* to *Strongly disagree* with *Somewhat agree/disagree* and a neutral choice in the middle. The practical view is that turning this scale into an ordinal numeric scale from 1 to 5 (see reference) and averaging the responses is helpful in decision making,[31] particularly when comparing different groups of responders.

Data models

More sophisticated decision-support tools applying data models facilitate speed, accuracy and consistency in decision making. These are generally automated or semi-automated processes based on statistical analysis of data sets and have grown in popularity with developments in machine learning and artificial intelligence.

Data models can be highly beneficial because they can remove human bias and allow the data to determine the decision. However, depending on the data sets used to develop and/or train the models, bias may be introduced during the process. In addition, many decision makers do not like 'black boxes' and there may be some pushback from less scientific-minded decision makers.

Should you meet pushback on the black box, here's a tip.

Rather than providing an answer that must be taken and acted on, provide a range from which the decision maker must choose a number to move forward with. Even if you keep the range narrow to limit the effect of the decision maker's choice, you are much more likely to get buy-in, as the decision maker is making a decision rather than having a decision forced on them.

Visualising data

Visualising data using bar graphs, pie charts and spider charts helps people see how one number relates to another. However, with modern data interfaces, much more sophisticated data visualisation is possible — for example, showing data across a geographic area. This could be sales data demographics or information about the geology or ecology of a location, for example. In some instances, there can be multiple layers of data that are aggregated at more macro levels and detailed at the micro level.

With good data quality control, access to such a decision support tool not only ensures that the most up-to-date information is available promptly to a decision maker; it can also assist in guiding the workflow for a decision within a broader management tool, such as a procurement system requiring multiple assessments and sign-offs for large procurements. Both will improve the speed and consistency of decision making. An additional benefit is it allows decision makers to have a greater appreciation of the interconnectedness and/or interdependence of different elements of the decisions they are making.

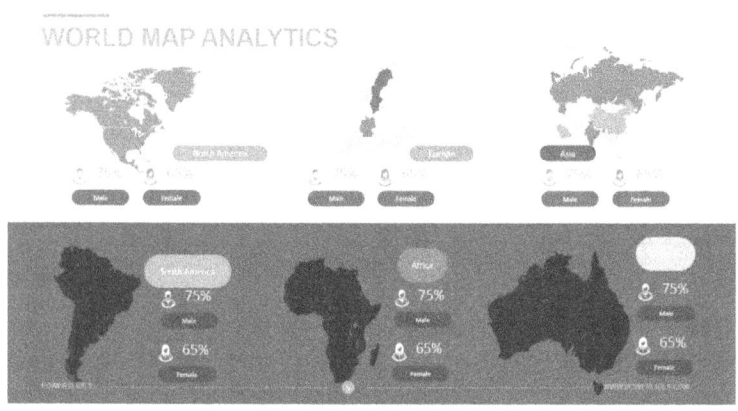

Figure 15: Example of visualisation of data (Source: PowerSlides)

> If you do your strategic planning well and maximise the likelihood of good-quality decision making, quickly and with implementation challenges fully in mind, you'll have set up the organisation for increased flow.

You now appreciate how decision process maps and decision support tools create flow in an organisation for recurring team decisions, including at the executive and board level. Now it is time to explore the types of strategic planning that lead to Type 1 decisions, like making your first acquisition, establishing your first international operation or launching a radically new product line. If you do your strategic planning well and maximise the likelihood of good-quality decision making, quickly and with implementation challenges fully in mind, you'll have set up the organisation for increased flow.

Chapter summary

There is a range of decision support tools you can utilise. I have provided you with examples of:

- decision trees — leading staff through a series of steps to reach a conclusion on the decision to make
- multi-criteria decision analysis (MCDA) — assisting staff to weigh up competing drivers of a decision
- risk assessment — developing simple risk scoring models to allow staff to assess risk quickly based on past experience of the team
- risk appetite — providing staff with clarity on the organisation's appetite for risk taking
- anonymous voting — a method for reducing bias and noise in team decisions
- data models — using data to build models to support key decisions
- visualising data — using visual representations to present data for decision making.

Part 3

Strategic or big-bet decisions

7

Go mental

How does your leadership team create value for the organisation? Can you easily articulate your answer? In short, you and your team create value by making great decisions to act or not act in pursuit of organisational purpose.

As I've already observed, your organisation is a complex system. And it is operating within a complex system. Neither can be controlled, which means your strategic decisions are often Type 1A decisions: they carry a high degree of risk and they are low on solid information. I have also pointed out that the value of a great strategic decision is equal to that of all the thousands upon thousands of subsequent decisions made during implementation. However,

> When we are determining our strategic stance for the next one, two, three, five years or more, we are looking at a kaleidoscope of possible pathways.

getting the big decisions right, the big-bet and complex ones, is where the value adding starts.

When we are determining our strategic stance for the next one, two, three, five years or more, we are looking at a kaleidoscope of possible pathways. That is, the pathways 'change before your very eyes' as you rotate your mind through different scenarios of how your world may pan out over time. As you stare into the kaleidoscope you may well become aware you are, figuratively speaking, facing the Uncertainty Paradox — that is, the only certainty is uncertainty!

I first wrote about the Uncertainty Paradox in *Risky Business: How Successful Organisations Embrace Uncertainty* (2021), where I declared grandly, 'the most successful organisations learn to systematically confront and get comfortable with uncertainty. They learn to embrace it. They face the drivers of their uncertainty, one by one.' My focus was to help organisations put into place a framework for driving risk-based decision making in relentless pursuit of delivering on the organisation's strategic objectives. However, the assumption was the organisation had determined the most optimal strategies available to it. This part of *Team Think* is about designing optimal strategies using mental models. Put another way, it's about designing your own future.

Mental modelling

I've always been aware of mental models and how you can frame a challenge or problem —for example, ask the question

'Does this follow the 80/20 rule where 80 per cent of X (e.g. sales) comes from 20 per cent of Y (e.g. customers)?' The 80/20 or Pareto Principle is a mental model.

Another example, although you might not have used this language, is scenario planning. When developing scenarios, you are developing mental models of the possible futures for your organisation from which you design a strategy that will address the most important aspects of the possible future. However, it is not the same as my Meta-Mental Model (MMM) approach to strategic decision making. Let me explain.

In their book *Six Faces of Globalization: Who Wins, Who Loses and Why It Matters* (2021), Anthea Roberts and Nicolas Lamp crafted six mental models of how different groups of people view who wins and who loses from globalisation. They call them the *establishment narrative*, the *left-wing populist narrative*, the *corporate power narrative*, the *right-wing populist narrative*, the *geoeconomic narrative* and the *global threats narrative*.

The establishment narrative proposes that everyone wins from globalisation because there is more economic pie to share around. The next four all have different winners and losers. For the left, the winners are the wealthy and the losers are the poor. For the right, winners are the countries to which jobs flow from richer nations, meaning the worker from richer nations loses out. For the corporate power narrative, big business wins, along with staff and shareholders, and everyone else loses. For the geoeconomic narrative, the view is that globalisation has strengthened some countries at the

> For the geoeconomic narrative, the view is that globalisation has strengthened some countries at the expense of strong nations like the US, leading to concerns over both economic and national security.

expense of strong nations like the US, leading to concerns over both economic and national security. One example is China's rapid economic ascendency, although it shows clear signs of a reversal in late 2023/early 2024, and the perceived siphoning of key technology from US academics, resulting in growing Chinese capabilities in artificial intelligence and military capability. Lastly, the global threats narrative suggests everybody loses because of the effect of globalisation on the planet — climate change and viral pandemics such as Covid, as well as economic ones such as the 2008 global financial crisis.

In developing these narratives, Roberts and Lamp set out to help readers develop a balanced world view and to influence strategic thinking. They point out that each of the narratives has merit and no one narrative deserves primacy. They use the various narratives to look at the pandemic and climate change to help explain the decisions made by various actors such as governments and business leaders. To share insights, they look at how the mental models on which each narrative was based can be used to show how actors can:

- switch narratives to suit their needs. It's not the fault of the wealthy — it's the poor countries stealing our jobs.

- hold the same views via overlaps between narratives. For President Trump, tariffs were needed to counter China's unfair trade practices. For President Biden, tariffs are a useful tool to help combat an aggressive China.
- choose different trade-offs. 'Saving lives through lockdowns to combat a pandemic is paramount' vs 'The cure (lockdowns and their economic cost and impact on mental health) will be worse than a more rapidly spreading virus'.
- have obvious biases. The US demands that all countries must submit to what it calls the 'global rules-based order', yet it chooses not to abide by authentic international laws that include the 2007 Convention on the Rights of Persons with Disabilities[32] and the 2008 Convention on Cluster Munitions.[33] The decision not to abide by the latter convention resulted in the deployment of US cluster munitions in Ukraine in 2023.

Roberts and Lamp suggest that a good understanding of these narratives and others from the perspective of regions such as Asia, South America and Africa will assist governments to develop better policies.

I agree and have built this in to my MMM approach to building strategies for big-bet and complex strategic decisions. I work with each member of an executive or other team to develop narratives based on their individual mental models of the world. For example, the Chief Finance Officer's world view and the Chief Customer Officer's world view will often differ. The mental models are analysed to identify patterns of overlaps, contradictions and trade-offs to help identify organisational strengths and opportunities as well as signs of bias and existential risks. Next, I assist the team to develop their team meta-mental model of the world in which they are operating and I work with them on designing the optimal strategy to deliver a successful outcome. This strategy will always require some level of flexibility, of course, since there is no certainty but uncertainty.

For longer-term decisions (such as for a strategic plan), meta-mental models allow you to evolve your strategy, because you can adjust settings within the model and see new patterns you need to address. If you don't, you risk coming up with narratives to explain what you see — then you stop looking. Following the meta-mental model approach, you find there are other narratives or bits of narratives that explain the same outcome. Patterns emerge and you can design strategies based on those patterns.

> Patterns emerge and you can design strategies based on those patterns.

Sometimes I hear people say that it's like scenario planning. Yes, there are commonalities, including the recognition of agents and drivers and key uncertainties. However, my approach differs in one critical way: the team's view of the future does not come from inferred views of each other's world view.

In the MMM method, each team member is asked to think about and document their world view in a narrative that is shared with all members of the team. From there you move to co-creation of the team's meta-mental model of the world, a powerful starting point for strategic decision making. And from there any number of approaches can be taken for the creation of an optimised strategy.

Team members also compare the approach to the development of 'persona' in the design of software applications, 'patient journeys' for the design of health facilities or 'empathy maps' of customers for the design of services. And they are right. There are similarities. The difference is the narratives are about the environment in which the persona, patients and customers exist.

A most insightful comment came from my friend and colleague, the futurist Alex Hagan. He said, 'That's interesting. It's like you are applying systems thinking to the team and systems mapping the team's decision making.' *Yes.* It came logically to me because of my training as a chemical engineer in which I learned the benefits of mapping very complicated processes.

Before I explain how to create your team's meta-mental model of the world, let me quote Kahneman et al. from *Noise*: 'When do you feel confident in a judgment? Two conditions must be satisfied: the story you believe must be comprehensively coherent, and there must be no attractive alternatives.' Meta-mental models deliver this.

Building narratives

My life partner, Jacquie, is the owner of My Life Story Writer, which specialises in helping clients transform their life stories into books. Her services are especially valuable for grandchildren who may be too young or preoccupied to ask important questions about their grandparents. By helping them to capture these stories, Jacquie ensures that future generations will have access to the answers they seek.

Jacquie has a unique way of collecting her clients' life in stories. She is so good at it she makes them cry. Literally. When her client, or more likely a close family member, first holds the printed book in their hands, they literally start to weep. She will get off the phone or finish reading an email and comment on how much they love the book. I always ask, 'Did they cry?' The answer has always been 'Yes'!

Many of her clients grow so fond of her during the experience that she and I are invited for dinner. One even invited us to stay at their holiday home. When that happens I invariably need to read their story before meeting them.

My favourite was of a man who was born in Western Australia, lived in a dirt-floor hut made from saplings covered in whitewashed hessian, and ended up owning property at the beach in Sydney. His rags-to-riches story included a cast of colourful characters and even more colourful stories that read like a novel!

I have long appreciated — and used — the power of storytelling. Reading these stories and quizzing Jacquie on her technique inspired me to come up with new methods for developing narratives of mental models for executives that would enhance the development of a meta-mental model of their strategy.

> I have long appreciated — and used — the power of storytelling.

Here, in very short form, is my technique for developing narratives of mental models of team members. It consists of a suite of narratives from which to develop the meta-mental model:

1. **Describe.** First you need to describe the big-bet decision so everyone is on the same page. Sometimes that will be clear — for example, whether or not to acquire a particular company or how much to bid for a company or asset that is up for sale. Another might be less concrete, such as, 'In which direction should we take the company next?'
2. **Frame.** Next you need to frame the decision. Is this decision about a growth strategy or is it about survival? Or is it about purpose and mission? Is it opportunistic or is it another stage of implementation of the grand plan?
3. **Baseline.** Ask each team member — the CFO, the COO and so on — whether their initial view of the decision leant towards a straightforward 'yes, it's a good idea' or a 'no'. Then use your AI app to write an article (say, 350 words) on why it is a good or bad idea

to decide one way or another from the perspective of that team member's job role.

4. **Create.** Working with the team member, get creative about what's possible, good and bad. This is where Jacquie's interview technique comes in. You will need to ask thought-provoking questions like, 'When in your career did you see X?' Or, 'What life experiences can you draw on to find parallels between life and this decision?' You can also ask your AI app for help.

5. **Narrate.** With the team member's input, develop a full narrative of the scenario, making sure to describe:

   a. key agents and their relationships to each other and to key drivers

   b. key drivers, including causal factors and causal mechanisms

   c. the 'scene', including location(s), agents who are protagonists and agents as partners

   d. the 'plot', which reflects the team member's fears and their optimism about the merit of the decision played out over a pre-agreed period, such as six months, twelve months, three years or more

   e. the 'moral of the story'.

Now you have the narratives, let's move on to developing your team's meta-mental model.

Chapter summary

Mental models are powerful in helping make sense of the world.

While mental models of recurring team decisions can be mapped to form a common view, mental models of the environment in which strategic, big-bet decisions are made are more easily articulated via narratives.

By developing narratives it is easier to see when people:

- switch narratives to suit their needs
- hold the same views via overlaps between narratives
- may opt for different trade-offs in the same situation
- have obvious biases towards one view of the world over another.

The starting point for using narratives to understand your environment and to build a compelling strategy for your organisation or a big-bet decision, is developing a suite of narratives with your team.

8

Go hard

I went to an all-boys high school dominated by Anglos with a mix of Eastern European, Greek, Italian and Lebanese kids. Oh, and one kid of Chinese descent we called Crackers, after Chinese crackers.

Racism was more common in those days than it is now. At school, if a schoolmate made a racist remark about Chinese people and was challenged with, 'But what about Crackers?' he would say, 'Not him. He's different. He's a mate', while looking uncomfortable.

This, of course, is an example of cognitive dissonance, the mental discomfort we may feel when holding two contrasting points of view at the same time. For example, in business, it might be found in bland marketing statements: 'We are all about the customer' while those responsible are fully aware customers are walking out the door due to poor customer service!

Developing meta-mental models requires a level of cognitive disruption to cast aside biases, noise and any cognitive dissonance of team members. A disruption the team must accept. Many of your team members' beliefs and even values are going to be challenged. That is why I titled this chapter 'Go hard'. There will be some confronting moments, but the outcome will be worth it.

> Developing meta-mental models requires a level of cognitive disruption to cast aside biases, noise and any cognitive dissonance of team members.

What is important is how each team member manages the experience. As their leader you must continually check yourself and remind them not to become advocates for a position. Each of you needs to sit back, take several breaths, open your mind to other possibilities and ask questions for a deeper insight into a narrative — all before you pass judgement.

Developing meta-mental models

A meta-mental model is one version of a balanced world view. The British statistician, George Box, is often quoted: 'All models are wrong, but some are useful.'[34] Your role is to make sure your model is compelling so it can be used in making your decisions about your future. What makes a meta-mental model compelling? Consider the interplay between your narratives, the patterns you find and your goals, as illustrated in figure 16.

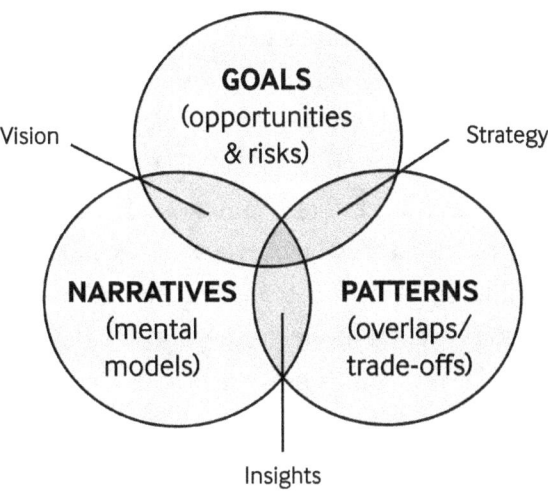

Figure 16: Meta-mental models

Having developed your team members' narratives, you need to apply them by switching elements in and out, overlapping them, identifying contradictions, mapping trade-offs, identifying shifts and articulating protagonists' blind spots. All these lead to the identification of critical patterns that need to be addressed. This is when cognitive disruption will be at its strongest as the different narratives of different team members interact and clash. The patterns you identify will give you the insights you need to see a vision of a bigger and brighter future so you can set audacious goals and make more informed decisions on your strategy to achieve them.

Overlaps, contradictions and trade-offs

Start with the agents and the drivers of each narrative that result in the moral of the story. For agents, it's about their views and their relationships with you and with each other. For drivers, it is the causal factors and mechanisms and the outcomes they derive. Which narratives have overlapping views on agents and drivers? What elements of different narratives can you switch in or out to create newly aligned narratives? Which narratives can you merge to form a new narrative? Now look for the overlaps between the new and the remaining old ones for strong agreement on agents and drivers of your mental model of the world.

Next look for contradictions. Which narratives have completely different views of agents and drivers of the moral of the story? Remember, don't judge; identify and find out more about the views of the narrator. Which contradictions can we solve now and which need further research and/or analysis? Which elements could be switched in or out to resolve a clash? How critical are the contradictions? If they are critical and will take time to resolve, they need to be parked and the contradictions allowed to continue as you work through new narratives.

Next identify trade-offs. There are classic ones, such as speed to market vs functionality in software applications or profit over customer satisfaction. Again, which elements can be switched in or out to resolve the trade-offs? Which narratives can you merge as they overlap? Which reveal contradictions you can look to resolve?

Shifts and blind spots

Let me lay out some more of the challenge for you. While

you are working on the overlaps, contradictions and trade-offs, also be on the lookout for how agents in your narratives either have shifted over time or have major blind spots. Let me give you an example.

Years ago I watched a documentary called, simply, *88* written by Adrian Russell Wills and Michaela Perske.[35] It tells the tale of the Indigenous Australians, some of whom travelled thousands of kilometres by minibus, truck and car, to a meeting in a town near Sydney in preparation for a convoy into Sydney to protest the Bicentennial celebrations on Australia Day 1988. It is a compelling story. The convoy was met, not with disdain and policy barriers, but with respect and recognition. There was much to celebrate, but most Australians knew that what the placards said was true: 'White Australia has a black history'.[36] In 1980 the Australian Bicentennial Authority was created through an Act of Parliament with the mission of finding a way to celebrate the bicentenary with sensitivity while building a stronger sense of what being Australian really meant. The authority proposed that the celebration 'be seen as a day of contact, not of conquest . . . the day which began the fusion of Australians'.[37]

I watched on YouTube then Labor Prime Minister Bob Hawke's Bicentennial Australia Day speech to see how he handled it. He did not mention the Indigenous people of Australia at all.

Wind forward twenty years to 2008 when Labor Prime

Minister Kevin Rudd stood up in Parliament to offer a formal apology to Australia's Indigenous peoples.

Wind forward a further fifteen years to 2023 and Labor Prime Minister Anthony Albanese delivered on an election campaign promise to hold a referendum on delivering an Indigenous Voice to Parliament that would be enshrined in the Constitution. The referendum failed. Pundits offered many reasons, but a frequent argument of the 'No' campaign was that the Voice would divide the nation, when 'we are all Australians'.

There was a great deal of nuance behind the decisions leading to these events. However, they demonstrate how the national narrative can and does shift over time.

Of course, most of the shifts and biases you will be looking for are not national ones. A good starting point for you and the team to identify shifts is to compare past and present performance. What's different? Perhaps there is a shift in attitudes among customers, suppliers or regulators. You don't need to be a rocket scientist to identify shifts in regulators — for example, the ramp up in power and regulations of the Australian Prudential Regulation Authority (APRA) as the regulator of the finance sector after the HIH Insurance royal commission. A change of Commissioner at Australia's competition regulator, the ACCC, often results in a shift of focus, as does a change in government!

Now is the time to finalise your meta-mental model, your MMM.

Your meta-mental model

As you have worked through analysing your team's narratives, merging them to form new ones and merging them again, you will have narrowed the field to just a few. If you have not been able to solve critical contradictions between narratives, you will find yourself with multiple narratives. However, I encourage you to keep merging until you have no more than four. That leaves one thing to do.

Before you work on your strategy or finalise your one-off strategic decision (such as on the amount to bid for an asset or takeover target) you need to assess risk vs reward for each remaining narrative.

To assess risk vs reward you need to articulate the key risks and opportunities for each narrative. Do your best to quantify them. Next, assess each narrative against your organisation's appetite for risk. When I discuss appetite for risk with a team, I sometimes use a surf lifesaving analogy.

> Before you work on your strategy or finalise your one-off strategic decision you need to assess risk vs reward for each remaining narrative.

It is drummed into Australian kids to 'swim between the flags'. At all our popular beaches surf lifesavers patrol and assess the condition of the beach each day, and set out the flags that define where it is safe to swim and to play. When the conditions are too rough, they close the beach and replace the flags with signs warning that the beach is closed due to, say, dangerous undercurrents. When the conditions are placid, they spread the flags a long way apart. When conditions are somewhat dangerous, they place the flags closer together, well away from dangers such as rips and rocks. Unfortunately for stronger swimmers, the lifesavers must set the flags to suit those less able.

For each narrative remaining, ask yourself and your team how capable you are of delivering the narrative. You won't yet have determined your strategy, but you will have a general feel for your ability to deliver. Now decide which surf lifesaving scenario describes each narrative's risk profile best — beach closed, flags far apart, flags close together or somewhere in between. If the beach is closed, that is a narrative your strategy must avoid. For those remaining, how do the opportunities weigh up? Is the riskiest narrative compelling or should you play safer?

Once you have agreed on the risk vs reward trade-off, you can set your goals for each strategy. For narratives for which appetite is high, the goals should be audacious. When appetite is low, but the opportunities are high, the short-term goals should be bite-sized. However, the longer-term goals can be as audacious as you like. If you choose bite-size chunks with your strategy, you will soon either become hungrier or decide to eat elsewhere!

Now you need to formulate the 'moral of the story' for each of your remaining scenarios, whether good, bad or indifferent. If you have one compelling narrative, this becomes your meta-mental model, and the moral of the story will guide you and the team as you work towards making it a reality. However, knowing that the only certainty is uncertainty, don't discard the other two or three narratives. You will need to plan, as best you can, for all of them.

Now you have gone hard with your thinking, it's time to go fast on decision making to determine your course of action, whether on a strategic plan or on the execution of a one-off strategic decision.

Before we move on to the next chapter, a word on facilitating the development of a meta-mental model of your world. As you can imagine, there is a knack to facilitating such an experience. While I won't go into all the nuances of that here, I will give you my top tip: *diverge before you converge.* Record on paper individual views on the overlaps, contradictions, trade-offs and shifts before bringing the ideas together.

> If you have one compelling narrative, this becomes your meta-mental model, and the moral of the story will guide you and the team as you work towards making it a reality.

Chapter summary

Developing meta-mental models requires the creation of a level of cognitive disruption so you and your team can question the veracity of your narratives.

Creating a meta-mental model requires you to create interplay between the narratives to find overlaps, contradictions, opposing trade-offs, shifts and blind spots of key protagonists.

The greatest benefit comes when merging narratives to form new ones and reducing them to a smaller range of possible futures.

Following this hard work, you are set to develop your strategy to optimally position your team for success, no matter what the world throws at you.

9

Go fast

What does it mean to go fast? It's a fair question. The story of the Bill and Melinda Gates Foundation's assistance in the assault on the poliovirus helps answer this for us.

> What does it mean to go fast?

In 1988 polio was paralysing 350,000 people every year. By 2007 the caseload had reduced to just 1,300 but stubbornly refused to fall further. Then the Gates foundation joined the fight. At the time of writing, the World Health Organization reported that 'Of the 3 strains of wild poliovirus (type 1, type 2 and type 3), wild poliovirus type 2 was eradicated in 1999 and wild poliovirus type 3 was eradicated in 2020. As at 2022, endemic wild poliovirus type 1 remains in two countries: Pakistan and Afghanistan.'[38] Just six cases were reported in 2021.

Bill Gates refers to the decision of the Foundation to go

all-out on polio as 'one of the riskiest ventures it's ever attempted'.[39] Sixteen years later the end goal is in sight.

Did they fail to move fast enough? In the same blog post, Gates writes:

> Ultimately, no matter how much analysis we do, I have to be comfortable with a lot of uncertainty. We are tackling problems where progress is measured not just in years but often decades — where your end goal doesn't change, but your path to get there might have to. The trick is to do whatever I can to keep learning and to be open to new and novel ways to bring us a step closer to our goals. That approach has guided every big bet I've made in my career from Microsoft to today — including polio.

He goes on to describe the pressure he felt to 'make every dollar and every day count', as well as the innovations in disease surveillance they funded to better target the disease and to improve the quality of the vaccination campaigns:

> The job is to keep moving forward, adjusting to the unexpected with new ideas and energy so we can reach the last unprotected child and achieve a polio-free world. That's a bet worth every dollar.

In reading the post, it was clear to me that to go fast on big-bet and complex strategic decisions is to act and learn. Here is the process I take teams through to set them up to act and learn. It's all about LIPS and Gates!

Hot LIPS

My mother was a *M*A*S*H* fanatic who was still watching reruns at 90 years of age! Who knows how many times she had seen each episode. Growing up, we had one television, and streaming services did not yet exist, and she often made the call on what was watched. Hence I know all the characters well, including Margaret 'Hot Lips' Houlihan!

If you don't know about the show, it was set in a US MASH unit (a mobile army surgical hospital) during the Korean War. Major Houlihan was a stickler for the rules but cared very passionately about saving lives and caring for the injured and the sick. These elements combined to form a perfect analogy for my acronym LIPS.

> LIPS stands for Leadership, Infrastructure, People and Systems. Without the right leaders you cannot achieve many or perhaps any of your goals.

LIPS stands for Leadership, Infrastructure, People and Systems. Without the right leaders you cannot achieve many or perhaps any of your goals. The wrong infrastructure, which includes your facilities and fleets, may cost extra time and potentially large sums of money. If you don't have the right people, it will take time to find and perhaps upskill them, and to build the culture required to deliver. And if you don't have the right systems in place, inefficiencies, errors and rework will escalate until you are forced to slow down, design and implement new systems.

A MASH unit had to do LIPS very, very well to be effective. The process was designed to have the infrastructure, people and systems of work in place fast. However, without passionate and thoughtful leaders like Major Houlihan as Head Nurse, they could not deliver on their potential.

A LIPS diagnostic tool is available in the free resources area of my website. I work with a team by taking them through the LIPS tool for each of the narratives to identify the gaps between the current organisational design and capacity, and what will be required to navigate each of those narratives.

Next we look for common gaps. As Bahar, Tan and Altintas explain in their paper 'A Strategic Approach for Learning Organizations: Mental Models', your job is to 'create channels between the problem and the mental model'.[40] For example, which gaps need new leaders or leadership development, which need infrastructure, which need people or their development, and which need systems upgrades, whether systems of work or system applications. I ask teams to estimate the cost and effort to plan and execute the gap fillers. Then we turn to my Quadrant Planning Model (QPM) (figure 17).

```
                    High Reward
                         ▲
                         │
            ┌─────────┐  │  ┌─────────┐
            │  PROBE  │  │  │  PLAN   │
            └─────────┘  │  └─────────┘
High Risk ◄──────────────┼──────────────► Low Risk
            ┌─────────┐  │  ┌─────────┐
            │  PARK   │  │  │  PICK   │
            └─────────┘  │  └─────────┘
                         │
                         ▼
                    Low Reward
```

Figure 17: Quadrant Planning Model

I ask the team to identify how many gaps each gap filler will resolve and to plot them on the model. As this model shows, the fillers that are easier to deliver and that will resolve the most gaps should be planned immediately, while those that are harder or will fill fewer gaps can be parked for now. Those in the top left quadrant need to be probed. Set up a plan to start working on them with the intention of determining the ones that can be delivered sooner — with most benefit — and those that are likely to be more difficult or that may prove to deliver less benefit so can be moved into the Park quadrant.

After these three quadrants have been dealt with, the team moves to the bottom right to 'pick' any gap fillers that should be planned now, because they will help complete the suite of actions that will best cover all the narratives. How sweet is that?

Gates

Despite the title of this chapter, sometimes we go too fast and falter. That is why I recommend the team adopt a version of the gateway approach favoured by governments when they are investing in big-bet projects. A typical set of gateways might look like this:

- Gate 1: Concept and feasibility or problem definition and solution
- Gate 2: Business case
- Gate 3: Readiness for market or pre-tender review
- Gate 4: Tender decision
- Gate 5: Readiness for service
- Gate 6: Benefits realisation or lessons learned.

I have not found a set of gateways that is generic enough to work for every implementation of big-bet and complex strategic decisions. The approach I take is to blend the Strategy Funnel approach I introduced in my book *Risky Business: How Successful Organisations Embrace Uncertainty*, with gateways at set times and with a good set of questions to ask. The result is my Strategy Funnel Mk II (figure 18).

As you can see from the diagram, planned, picked and probing actions are put into play and metaphorically poured into the funnel. At a pre-agreed time for the nature, size and complexity of the entire strategic program, each is assessed against updated narratives, the gaps that need filling and the likelihood the actions taken will successfully fill the gap. Some are jettisoned from the program (funnel) while others undergo significant modification. The same process is followed at subsequent gateways at agreed times.

Did you pick up on the implications for your narratives? I referred to 'updated narratives'. That's right, at each gateway you and your team revisit the narratives to see how they have changed. What has become a reality, what is more likely to, and what aspects of the narrative have disappeared or become less likely?

And what does all this mean? This step is not to be treated lightly. The tendency is to undercook it because of the implications. The unspoken thoughts might be 'It might make us look stupid' or 'I don't want to undo so much of this good work; we will make it work'.

Facing up to the reality of changes in circumstances or changes in your appreciation of the aspects of the narratives is paramount to your success!

Which reminds me: part of going fast is to set up signals that allow you to recognise your narratives are shifting.

> Facing up to the reality of changes in circumstances or changes in your appreciation of the aspects of the narratives is paramount to your success!

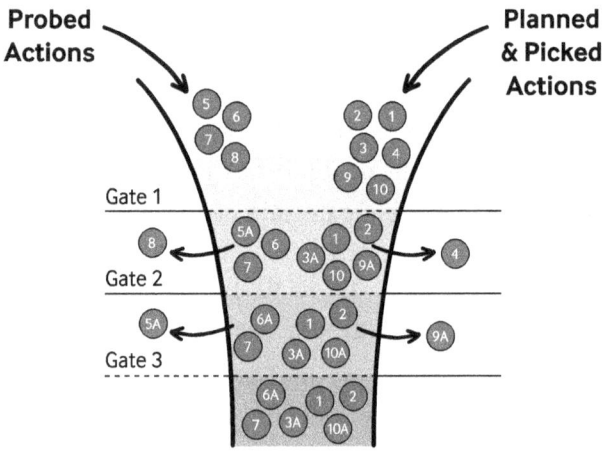

Figure 18: The Strategy Funnel Mk II

Signals

In *Risky Business*, in a chapter called 'Reading the signals', I introduced the Strategy Funnel and took the reader through the importance of developing Key Risk Indicators to provide early indications of risk to future performance. The same principles apply to big-bet and complex strategic decisions, except the funnel is focused less on risk and more on areas of key assumptions and drivers.

A colleague of mine, Dr Andrew Pratley, has started using the doomsday clock analogy, introduced in the *Bulletin of Atomic Scientists* in 1947, to express the dangers of imminent global calamity.[41] In late 2023, the clock stood at 90 seconds to midnight, the closest it has ever been.

We use this analogy to talk about the difference between Key Risk Indicators of convenience and ones that are transformational for organisations because of the early warning delivered and the reliability of the measures. This allows an organisation to be agile rather than taking last-minute, costly and time-consuming actions.

The secret to high-quality signals for your meta-mental model narratives is to identify a potentially excellent measure, develop a hypothesis on how that measure will change, given changes in key drivers, then test it.

The secret to identifying the best signals to measure is quality facilitation. I've found that an experienced facilitator is able to dig deeper into a team's thinking than they would themselves.

The secret to preparing good hypotheses, as I found out working with Andrew Pratley, is to understand there are only three questions to ask, and to ask them a number of times, to get the hang of it. The three questions are: Is this a question of . . .

1. Probability — how likely is something to occur, or how frequently?
2. Relationships — how does one thing relate to another?
3. Differences — how does one thing differ from another?

For example:

- H1: 50 per cent of our profits come from 20 per cent of our customers — Probability.
- H2: Our clients' acceptance of fees is independent of our profit margin — Relationships.
- H3: New staff who don't fit into our culture are more likely to be bullied by their managers than new staff who fit into our culture — Differences.

Once you have a good hypothesis, your team will need to follow an appropriate process to design and test it. The problem that comes up most commonly is a lack of data. All that means is the design of your test needs to create data. Concerning hypothesis H3, for example, there is likely no measure of a person's cultural fit that is tracked from day one through to their departure. Working with the right subject-matter experts, you could design and track such a measure.

My final word on signals is to please, please, please move beyond the convenient and set up the early warnings that will allow you to adjust early and often to changing narratives.

Doubling down

Another concept I introduce to some clients is one I picked up from working with teams designing critical safety software, such as the software running the train system. Doubling down is establishing two separate teams to work on the same solution. For larger companies this can be a great strategy for succeeding with your entire analysis and solution process or just for your projects in the Probe quadrant of my planning model, projects that are important but are looking hard.

The broad concept is that you allow the teams to run completely independently, and you check in on them at set intervals until there is a clear 'winner'. That is not necessarily the best way to look at it, unless you want to make it more competitive than it may have naturally been. A better approach is to look at it as 'fail fast and fail often' and we will find a way.

Another form of doubling down to 'go fast' is what has been coined the *pressure cooker analogy* of organisational performance. That is, the best performance comes when you turn up the heat on teams while maintaining a functioning pressure relief valve. If you overheat things, the pressure built up is quickly released back to an acceptable level. Typically this is an intervention such as a brief 'shutdown' while everyone goes home or takes time out for some rest and recuperation. In my experience there is one critical element you should add to your pressure relief valve. Continually remind your teams of the values of the organisation. It is not at all unusual that teams under pressure find ways to get things done only to regret, with a capital R, what they have

> Another form of doubling down to 'go fast' is what has been coined the *pressure cooker analogy* of organisational performance.

done. This may sometimes have ramifications all the way to the CEO and Chair of the Board.

I've taken you through my process for tackling strategic or big-bet decisions using mental models and the narratives you can form around them. Please remember, you won't ever know whether or not you made optimal decisions. All you can do is follow a good process diligently and get moving. The rest of your success will come from your talented team of creative, connected and purpose-driven people. Trust them.

Part 4 is about helping you and your team succeed in all those other moments of team decision making. Many times the team will make decisions around delivering your strategy. No matter the quality of your team, there will always be a tendency for bias and noise to affect judgement. So I aim to give you a better understanding of the risks involved in team decision making and how best to deal with them.

Chapter summary

Going fast is better known as fail fast. That is, act and learn and act again.

Effective strategy implementation requires great leadership, good infrastructure, committed people and efficient and effective systems. Identify the gaps in these and the strategic initiatives, or gap fillers, that will have most impact on your strategy.

Categorise strategic initiatives into those that should be planned immediately, parked, probed or picked for further development to prioritise your limited resources.

Use gateways to test initiatives and fail them fast or accelerate them.

Narratives need to be updated based on signals that key drivers have changed.

Mission critical initiatives should have two independent teams developing solutions until one, or none, proves successful.

Part 4

Decision hygiene

10

The unmaking of strategic decisions

I've explained that purpose, talent and connectedness are key to a team's quality decisions. And you will be aware of the power of a wonderful team. Guess what, as Ricardo Vargas calls out in his 2021 book, *Chief Executive Team*, the elephant in the room is that the most important team in your organisation is the executive team, yet most are not functioning as a team. Working with executive teams, Vargas runs an exercise in which he asks each executive to write the names of their team members on cards. Of course, they write down the team members who work *for* them, not their executive-team colleagues.

Vargas identifies many reasons why executive teams do not function well. Here are just three:

- Many are competing to be the next CEO.
- They are all fighting for budget.

- One or more are underperforming, impacting the rest of the organisation.

While these reasons are not exclusive to the executive team, they become bigger issues and more impactful the higher the team sits in the organisation. The executive team is where ambition and big egos clash.

Vargas also made me aware of a 2019 *Harvard Business Review* article by Neal Kissel and Patrick Foley that found new CEOs are often surprised by how different the role is compared with what they had expected.[42] The surprise stemmed from:

- the time required to address or solve issues with direct reports, poor functioning governance committees, poor reporting and escalation of trivial issues
- the effort required to manage board and other external relationships
- the challenge of making decisions with less knowledge of the issues than when they were leading only a segment of the organisation.

I hope that as you read those three items you thought about flow, decision process maps and decision support tools. They will address many of these challenges. But not all big-bet decisions still need to be made in the most well-orchestrated organisations. So decision hygiene, as Kahneman et al. call it in *Noise*, needs to be a focus.

As I explained back in chapter 1, Kahneman et al. point out

that ineffectual or poor team decision making is exacerbated by a combination of bias and noise, bias suggesting a tendency to cling to certain preconceived beliefs while noise is about inconsistency between decision makers or by the same decision maker at a different time or place. I deal with each separately below.

Common types of bias

Here I list some of the more commonly occurring and understood cognitive biases to give you a feel for why good decision-making processes are so important. For a deeper understanding of these biases, I recommend Kahneman's *Thinking Fast and Slow*. Or you could just google a list — be careful, it could do your head in!

> We are more likely to take the view of someone we trust or admire than of the person most qualified to give their opinion.

- *Affect bias.* We are more likely to take the view of someone we trust or admire than of the person most qualified to give their opinion.
- *Anchoring bias.* We anchor to the first thing said, particularly if it is by the team leader. The more some of the team anchor to the first thing or the first few things said, the less likely others are to raise alternative points of view. This is referred to by Sunstein and Hastie in *Wiser* as 'amplifying' the initial error.

- *Availability bias.* We judge the likelihood of something happening based on our experience of it. It happened to us, so it happens all the time.
- *Confirmation bias.* We subconsciously search our memory for, or inadvertently only hear evidence from, new sources that confirm the first position we take on an issue or our initial impressions, which lead to our first position. We hold on to our position even in the face of contrary evidence.
- *Fundamental attribution error.* This is a tendency to identify a firm cause for a person's behaviour when it could be explained by many other potential circumstances.
- *Peak-end bias.* We remember most clearly the last significant statement or event over all the preceding ones. For example a keynote speaker with a great ending will score higher in evaluation surveys than a keynote whose peak points were much earlier in their presentation.
- *Planning fallacy.* Despite all the evidence of previous projects, we decide this time it is going to be different! That is, we are so very optimistic at times.

I'm sure many, if not all, of these resonate with you. Now to one other bias that is not as commonly talked about: organisational bias, or the way culture and organisational design can affect how decisions are made.

Organisational bias

While groupthink is about group dynamics and the desire to conform so the group remains of like mind, it risks resulting in the avoidance of challenging the critical thinking of the group. There is another phenomenon at play that I call organisationthink, through which the culture of an organisation influences how a decision is implemented.

The effect of organisational culture on decision making was powerfully driven home for me when I read *Essence of Decision: Explaining the Cuban Missile Crisis* (2nd edition) by Graham Allison and Philip Zelikow. You may find the book a challenge to read, but the lessons it offers are important.

Allison and Zelikow look at decision making during the crisis through three lenses: (1) the rational actor, (2) organisational behaviour and (3) governmental politics. Most people are familiar with rational decision making and the effects of politics, but are less so with the effect of organisational behaviour. In short, leaders make decisions and staff implement them, which requires them to interpret meaning and to identify means of achieving perceived goals. Unless teams are at the top of the quality decision-making ladder (figure 4) where they are (a) strongly aligned on purpose, (b) full of talent and (c) synchronous as a team, their interpretation and choice of methods of implementation are not always what the leader has in mind. There can be no better example than Khrushchev and the Soviet military machine during the Cuban Missile Crisis.

The Soviet mission was ostensibly a secret operation — the US was not supposed to know. But when the Soviets built missile bases in Cuba, they did not camouflage them from the air. Why? Allison and Zelikow suggest it was because the Soviet forces responsible implemented as they had always implemented — according to the manual. The decision had been made not to camouflage bases in the Soviet Union to aid speed of deployment — that is, agility was chosen over secrecy. When it came to the deployment in Cuba, the message did not get through that this deployment was to be different.

> If the need for change is not identified and managed, the initiative is likely to fail or at least to be heavily impaired.

The lesson for senior leaders in organisations is the importance of understanding organisational culture when making a decision, in order to understand whether you will have good flow from the outset or if work will need to be done to build stronger teams. If the need for change is not identified and managed, the initiative is likely to fail or at least to be heavily impaired.

Now for the factors causing noise in decision making.

Common factors causing noise

Here I provide a high-level overview of the factors causing noise. For a deeper understanding of the individual factors and nuances, I recommend reading *Noise*.

- *Dichotomies.* If conflicting opinions are not managed through a constructive conversation, people will tend to defend their position more and more strongly, to the point of extremism. Consider US politics in recent years.
- *Different Scales.* We both believe a piece of information is significant, but one of us feels it overrides other factors while the other does not. Our scales of 'highly insignificant' to 'highly significant' are simply different. We establish risk criteria so when someone calls a risk 'high' it has to reflect the criteria.
- *Multiple Personalities.* We can make different decisions based on our mood, which can be affected by an infinite number of causes. Broadly, they can be categorised as times when we feel angry, stressed, tired, impatient, good or elated.
- *Social Influence.* 'The way we do things around here' reduces the likelihood of someone posing an alternative view. For example, we don't let younger staff run with projects, because when we have done so it has not turned out well. Most likely they lacked the experience to take the lead on that particular project and the situation is in no way representative.
- *Unshared Information.* Sometimes a team member will have information that does not support their views and they may be reluctant to share it. Or, because so much other information is being shared,

they don't want to burden the team, but it turns out the information was very important!

Here I have shared the views of some world-renowned experts. My biggest takeaway from *Wiser* (2014), *Noise* (2021) and *Chief Executive Team* (2021), on how to improve team thinking is that there is no silver bullet. You can't flick a switch and have everyone in the right frame of mind, carefully aggregating opinions, using circuit breakers to halt fatigue or draw out unshared information, with strong feedback loops running hot. It is up to teams to create the environment for this to occur. Let me help you help your team create the right environment.

> You can't flick a switch and have everyone in the right frame of mind.

As I noted at the beginning, I have studied decision making for a very long time. Over the next few chapters I will share with you a few models to help you ask penetrating questions of yourself and the team during decision making. I will explain the importance of some key roles in teams and help the team think like Einstein. This will guide you to identify and counter bias and noise in your team's decisions.

Chapter summary

The most important team in your organisation is the executive team and most executive teams do not function as a team.

New CEOs are often surprised by poor decision flow.

There are many sources of individual and team bias that can affect team decision making.

Organisational bias is the way culture and organisational design can affect how strategy implementation decisions are made.

Common factors causing noise are *dichotomies, differing value scales,* and our *multiple personalities* based on our mood, social influence and unshared information.

11

Leading by asking

Here you are, well on top of understanding how to establish terrific flow in your organisation. Now imagine two situations. In the first, you are about to decide a key element of your strategy for the next three years. In the second, the flow in your organisation has resulted in a major decision being appropriately escalated to the executive team for determination.

As CEO or team leader, you have tremendous influence over the quality of the decision in both these circumstances. To what extent is it your decision or the team's decision? If yours, how much are you willing to listen to information and opinion from your team members before making the decision? If it's to be the team's decision, are you looking for consensus or are you happy to go with the majority or average of all opinions? Perhaps you are willing to delegate the authority to decide to one of your team members.

Here are three rules of thumb to consider when making these choices:

- *Rule 1: You are not smarter than the group.* Reserve decisions that need little or no consultation to those that require speed and do not impact significantly on the team or organisation.
- *Rule 2: Consensus is great, but it's hard to achieve true consensus.* Where it is most important is in setting strategy so everyone on the team is clear on purpose, is keen to work creatively and will collaborate in sync towards achieving it. Because reaching consensus is difficult, break up your strategy and get consensus on all the elements you can. Then see rule 3.
- *Rule 3: Great teams love being averaged!* That is, great teams know that for highly uncertain and impactful elements of your strategy, the best decision is highly likely to be the average of everyone's views. For example, when deciding on the price you should bid in a competitive tender, do some anonymous voting! For voting on a yes/no or go/no-go decision, the average is the majority. If you have an even number of team members, identify which individual has most knowledge of the question to be decided before the vote, so if there is a tie their vote decides.

Now you have decided how the decision is going to be made, here are four of my decision support tools for you and your team to use. The Why Model, the Drivers Model, the Think Model and the Player Model will help you and the team ask good questions to identify any potential errors in the decision-making process.

The Why Model

The Why Model (figure 19) boils down the reason for failed strategic decisions to one of three things:

- *Clarification* — a lack of understanding of the strategic initiative decided on
- *Motivation* — asking the wrong question. Have we asked the most important question? Do we truly understand 'why' we want to take on this strategic initiative?
- *Implementation* — an overestimate of our capability to implement the initiative.

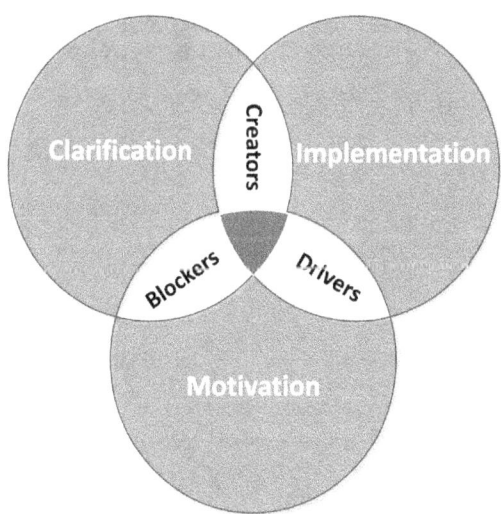

Figure 19: The Why Model

Let me take you through these, starting with implementation and working backwards.

Implementation

Teams are often distracted and fail to stay focused until a decision is fully implemented. They also tend to overestimate organisational capability in the first place. Sometimes, however, it is worse than that.

> Teams are often distracted and fail to stay focused until a decision is fully implemented.

A team's default decision-making stance is often to start by considering how to implement the 'great' idea just put forward. They ask themselves, 'How are we going to pull this off?' They have failed to clarify what the strategic initiative is really all about and whether they have the creative teams, working synchronously with clarity of purpose, to succeed.

The question to ask is, *'Have we gone straight to implementation without considering possible alternatives or clarifying what the idea really entails?'*

Clarification

We have all heard of analysis paralysis. Risk-averse organisations tend to over-analyse, while risk takers tend to under-analyse. Clarification efforts can result in misinformation or misunderstanding of the strategic initiative because of mental blockers created by our motivation — for example, wanting something, such as outdoing a competitor, way too much.

The questions to ask are:

- *Have we achieved sufficient clarification, and have we fully taken into account the challenges of implementation?*
- *What potential mental blockers may have affected the analysis?*

Motivation

The right kind of contained motivation can enhance our implementation efforts. On the other hand, motivation can create mental blockers that will adversely influence our decision making. More important, we have to ensure that we have the right motivation, that we are answering the right question, and that we have the right 'why' for the strategic initiative.

> The right kind of contained motivation can enhance our implementation efforts.

The questions to ask are:

- *What are the drivers of our motivation?*
- *What then is the real question we need to answer?*

To see how this might work in practice, consider this headline-grabbing decision.

The Australian Taxation Office (ATO) identified an issue they wanted to address. Some staff were not recording their work hours accurately. Some were leaving work early or having long lunches or a nice long read of the paper over breakfast after they got to work. What was the ATO's 'great idea'? To send out a memo urging staff to report anyone behaving in this way. Staff are the ones in the know, so this would be the fastest and most efficient way to tackle the problem, right?

Having gone straight to implementation in December 2017, the ATO decision makers woke up one morning in February 2018 to this headline by the (taxpayer-funded) Australian Broadcasting Corporation (ABC): 'ATO urges staff to dob in colleagues who take long lunches, read paper at work'.[43] In Australia to 'dob' means to 'rat' on them. Dobbing is seen as a very, very un-Australian thing to do, especially to a workmate, given our working-class heritage, which pitted workers against bosses.

If you had been an adviser to the ATO decision makers and you had utilised the thinking behind the Why Model, your line of commentary, questioning and advice would have gone something like this:

- *Implementation.* Seems quick and easy to implement, but can we take a little time to clarify what the impact might be?
- *Clarification.* I understand the ATO is anti-fraud and all about personal integrity. However, there are other fundamentals in play here, workplace trust being

one of them. If we start investigating individual staff, what impact do you think this might have on trust within and across teams? How else might we discover the worst offenders without compromising trust in the workplace?
- *Motivation*. Giving this some more thought, let's go back to the source issue. Is it about productivity or integrity and fraud? If the former, there are plenty of options for improving productivity among less-motivated staff — from working with team leaders to increase motivation, to introducing organisation-wide productivity competitions. If it's about integrity and fraud, the first place to start is by looking to influence those who may be offending but who don't recognise the ethics of their behaviour and may not appreciate the impact it has on their work colleagues. This may well apply to the majority of offenders. We can then move to Plan B for those who continue to offend.

Now for a model that will help you and the team understand the drivers of your motivation, so you are more confident you have the right 'why' for strategic decisions.

The Drivers Model

As we have established, we can all suffer blind spots caused by a range of psychological phenomena. What is behind them is at the intersection of our values, our environment and our genes (figure 20).

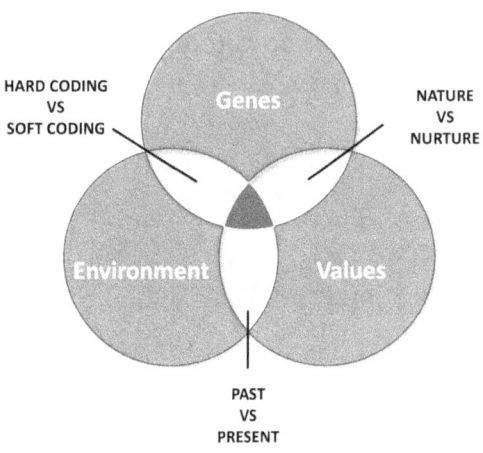

Figure 20: The Drivers Model

Whenever you are thinking about and looking to make a decision, your subconscious is grappling with what is genetically encoded in your brain, by what has been instilled in you by your carers and support network, by past experience and by what you are experiencing right now.

Your *genetic coding* prompts you to be wary of people who are different from you. You feel most comfortable in the bosom of your tribe, with the people you trust. They are the people you will listen to ahead of 'the smartest person in the room'.

Your *values* guide you towards being a good person and thriving within your tribe. Values are used to guide your decision making, and the tribe's values will be used to judge you in retrospect.

Your *environment* affects both your genetic coding and your value set. A strong and supportive tribe will affect your decision making differently from one that is under pressure, with cracks appearing in relationships. Ever worked in an underperforming team under pressure from without and from within?

To use this model with the team to assess the quality of your decision making, ask these questions:

- *How is the current environment affecting our thinking? How would we have felt about this decision six months or a year ago? What would we have decided then? What has changed? What mental blockers might that have created?*
- *Is this decision in line with our values? Would it pass the pub test? What would your mum say?*

Now to a model to help you identify any potential errors in the decision-making process, the Think Model.

The Think Model

The Think Model breaks down team thinking and deciding by process and by bias sets. In figure 21, the vertical axis helps you consider how the thinking started and how it concluded. The horizontal axis helps you consider how the information available and the discussion may have been biased.

In the four quadrants of the model are four of the most

common occurrences in a team discussion: Anchoring to the first few comments, a polarising discussion, amplification of any biases arising from the anchoring that then crowds out the sharing of further information.

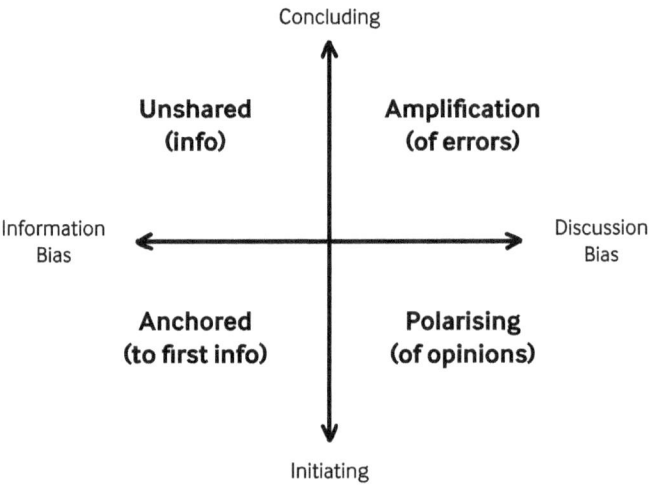

Figure 21: The Think Model

Two questions to ask using this model are:

- *How was the meeting initiated? Did I as the CEO/team leader put my opinions forward first? Did I seek alternative views or did I advocate for a single particular view? When alternative views arose, did I ensure the conversation was robust and constructive and not polarising?*
- *When concluding the discussion, did I make sure everyone had contributed something significant? Did*

I ensure a last opportunity to consider possible mental blockers that could have led to poor thinking?

Now to one more model and one more question to ask.

The Player Model

All the models above are decision-support tools. This one (figure 22) is a bit different. It helps you identify players on your team who are suited to unbiased, less noisy, strategic decision making, and those who might benefit from some coaching or mentoring.

The model suggests you should look at your team members in terms of their ability to collaborate, their emotional intelligence and their competitive spirit. Let me explain by discussing each of the three intersections of the model.

Figure 22: The Player Model

Allows effective processing

You need strong collaborators who will help each other to understand the complex world you are navigating and to develop strategies to get there. Strong collaborators with high emotional intelligence will be better able to connect and understand where others on the team are coming from, which will permit more effective processing of the information brought to the table.

Resistant to triggers

You want team members who are ambitious, who cultivate high standards and expect to be duly rewarded, but who also understand that being overly competitive can be detrimental to the team. Highly emotionally intelligent, they are also able to navigate robust discussions in which dissenting views do not lead to a polarised team. They resist the triggers that would lead others to 'dig their heels in' and hold firm at high cost.

Avoidance of bias

It is impossible to leave all your accumulated values, environment and gene-driven baggage at the door and erase all bias from the room, especially since most bias is unconscious. However, team members who are more than happy to collaborate and who strike a balance between the desire to win and the fear of being seen as second rate will bring a lot less bias to the table.

Let's now check out some of the key roles played when making big decisions.

Chapter summary

Not all decisions should be made by you.

I provide a series of models you can learn about to help your team understand and create the environment you all need for great decision making:

- The Why Model addresses the 'why' behind taking a strategic initiative.
- The Drivers Model helps your team explore blind spots to their thinking.
- The Think Model helps you assess the quality of a team's discussion.
- The Player Model identifies team members best suited to strategic decision making.

12

Role play

Every team member has a role to play when it comes to team decision making. However, there are a few important roles that need highlighting for different teams. Play along with me here as they are Chair of the Board, Commander-in-Chief, Chief Risk Officer, Chief Safety Officer and Chief Cynic.

Chair of the Board

As you can imagine, I have met a few Chairs in my time. Most have been very good, some simply outstanding. I come from the point of view of an adviser presenting my findings to the board. The outstanding ones are close to on time with every agenda item and across

> Every team member has a role to play when it comes to team decision making. However, there are a few important roles that need highlighting for different teams.

the pre-reading. They read the room well, facilitate robust discussion and know how to move people on when they are getting bogged down. They are also very good at articulating the decision made if required to do so by the board.

In early 2023, as I was writing this book, I attended a seminar titled 'Rethinking Governance & the Role of Boards'. Two Australian business titans, David Gonski AC and Zia Qureshi were keynote speakers. They were there to discuss and explore Fred Hilmer's recently released book *What's Wrong with Boards: Rethinking Corporate Governance* (2022). You couldn't find much more expertise on the subject than that offered by these three business leaders.

I was not disappointed on the evening of the seminar. I listened closely, bought Hilmer's book and read it with great interest, partly from the point of view of my role in advising boards, but also to see what I could identify for inclusion in *Team Think*.

The book is full of practical advice and of insights on decision making at board level. And while the focus is on public company boards, there is plenty to learn no matter the type of oversight body. Here are some of my key takeaways to help you, as a Chair, CEO or adviser, to ensure the right person is playing the right role to help guarantee the best decisions are made for your organisation:

- Hilmer critiques the skills matrix for board directors in the Governance Institute of Australia's Good Governance Guide, noting there is 'no mention about sound judgement, independence of thought, strong ethics or interpersonal skills — arguably four of the most important skills of any public company director'.

- He lists the following seven issues that must be addressed to drive performance: 'more rigorous selection of chairs; improving the role clarity of the chair; choosing the right directors; skills of an effective chair; the chair's role in providing the board with relevant, high-quality information; developing a nose for potential trouble; and setting the pace and ambition of change from the chair'.

- He refers to INSEAD research on the Chair's role, which suggests that in addition to not being a dominant voice or acting like the CEO, the Chair should help the board 'practise teaming', but adds, rather than the team analogy for boards, a more useful one to help understand their role and leadership is that of a group of judges led by a Chief Justice. Each judge brings an independent perspective, which can lead to split decisions or dissents as well as unanimous decisions.

- When listing some of the soft skills required of a Chair he includes: 'Creating tough, honest, harmonious and constructive discussions' and 'Sensitivity to values and culture'.

Now to the role of Commander-in-Chief.

Commander-in-Chief

Commander-in-Chief, CEO, Commissioner and Secretary are all titles representing the top dog in different types of organisations. In the previous chapter I laid out my core guidance for you no matter your title. I now want to single out some advice I have gleaned from clients of mine who have these titles.

Command and control environments

If you lead an organisation with a strong command and control environment, as you might find in the military and emergency services, you are likely very aware that what you say goes. Your greatest skill must be ensuring you are not first, second or even third to speak. Despite people looking to them for their view, the best leaders I have worked with let everyone else go first, sometimes explicitly asking them for their views.

Ministerial environments

If you head a government agency and report to a minister, you will be well aware of the challenge of working with the Minister's Office. A key finding by Graham Allison and Philip Zelikow when analysing the Cuban Missile Crisis, was that information is massaged as it makes its way through an organisation to the very top of political power. If I were you, I would be using the Why Model and the Drivers Model to assess the information that has been massaged on its way to you, and how what is conveyed to the Minister's Office may be further massaged. Are we answering the right question, and what are the drivers, and therefore the potential mental blockers, of those involved? And think about how the Minister may further massage the information for Cabinet.

Advisory boards or committees

If you have an advisory board or committee you could ignore, never do so. The best I have seen treat them as a true oversight board. Make sure, however, to co-create the mental model of the role of the advisory board or committees into a decision process map, to identify bottlenecks and decision support tools to ensure you receive good advice with minimal bias and noise.

Chief Risk Officer

Who is your Chief Risk Officer (CRO)? Why have you appointed one, and where do they sit in your organisation? These are interesting questions for many a CEO.

If you are in the finance sector in Australia, you should be able to answer these questions easily. The Australian Prudential Regulation Authority (APRA) prescribes via a prudential standard that the CRO must have a direct reporting line to the CEO and must be 'involved in, and have the authority to provide effective challenge to, activities and decisions that may materially affect the institution's risk profile'.[44] In my experience that means the CRO is on the executive team. APRA also prescribes that the CRO can't be the CEO or CFO and must be independent of any of the lines of business.

While APRA has done a heap of good in improving the management of risk and hence the management of organisations it regulates, I am not 100 per cent behind their required approach. The best CROs are trusted advisers to the executive team. They help the executive team think things through by bringing great research and analysis and by asking a bunch of critical questions. This reduces the likelihood of a horrendous decision to near zero and markedly improves the likelihood of the desired outcomes from the decision made. Their advice and the way they challenge the thinking of the team is highly valued.

Unfortunately, much of the guidance and language of APRA's standards and those of the Institute of Internal Auditors' Three Lines Model of risk management, which are called up by APRA in its standards, are counterproductive to the CRO being seen as a trusted adviser. The problem can be summed up in a few loaded words — think *oversight, challenge, compliance* and *assurance*.

> The problem with oversight is that it suggests the business decision makers are at best not sufficiently competent, and at worst would choose to do the wrong thing.

The problem with oversight is that it suggests the business decision makers are at best not sufficiently competent, and at worst would choose to do the wrong thing. The problem with challenge is that senior leaders like their thinking to be challenged when they are proven right, but not so much when they are proven wrong. Compliance and assurance make the CRO seem very much like the people from audit. The result: the people from the risk and compliance functions get tagged as BPOs or Business Prevention Officers.

Good CROs work around this as best they can. However, as I advised one APRA-regulated CRO recently, don't make it harder for yourself than it needs to be. The team are tasked with investigating breaches, which means they are a corporate cop. Who has the corporate cop as their trusted adviser? Not too many on the executive team, in my experience!

Also, in my experience, most other organisations do not have a CRO on the executive team. Including APRA where the CRO reports directly to the executive board along with the Chief Audit Executive, which clearly puts them outside the tent of the executive team.

If your view of the risk management function is not a positive one, or if the function does not exist, my advice to you is to gain a better understanding of the benefits of good risk management. You will find my book *Risky Business: How Successful Organisations Embrace Uncertainty* a useful resource. Next, put into place a management model that positions the risk managers as advisers to the business and elevates the position of the most senior risk person to executive level. Initially they may wear two hats, but over time you may want a dedicated CRO. Here is an example of exactly that shift.

Aged care provider, HammondCare, went from no senior risk management professional in 2019 to a dual role Chief Operating and Risk Officer in 2021, to a Chief Risk Officer in 2023. This evolution was driven in part by the appointment as CEO of Mike Baird, who came from the banking industry, and in part by the flow of regulation coming down the path for the industry following a royal commission into the aged care sector.

Chief Safety Officer

Here I mean psychological safety. Everyone in the room, whether or not they are on the executive team, should feel comfortable in voicing their opinion.

A lack of psychological safety arises when you or others on the executive shoot the messenger, react with anger on hearing of a mistake made or berate people in any way. Such behaviour creates high degrees of emotion among those affected and those observing, who react by putting up barriers to defend themselves and seek safety. They don't speak up. They hold on to, even hide, bad news or their own views on a decision. Wrongful actions by those in positions of power fracture an organisation's culture.

> Whose job is it to act as Chief Safety Officer? As CEO or team leader, it's yours. End of story.

Whose job is it to act as Chief Safety Officer? As CEO or team leader, it's yours. End of story. Figure 23 helps remind you of this.

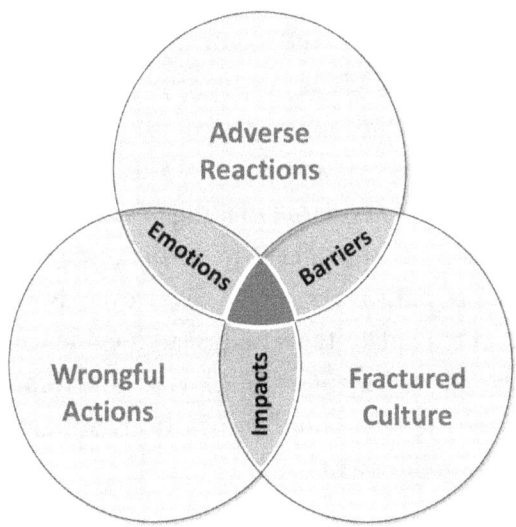

Figure 23: Psychological Safety

Chief Cynic

A number of authors have written about members of a decision-making team purposefully taking on the role of what I call the Chief Cynic. A heads up: this is not the CRO. The CRO is about providing insights, not about taking a questioning role, as a cynic might.

For example, in *What's Wrong with Boards* Hilmer refers to 'black hat directors'. His research found that some boards find value in purposefully assigning one or two directors to the role with the aim of asking uncomfortable questions. Without this explicit role, Hilmer suggests, a director might not ask these questions for fear of sounding negative or ignorant or in any other way deficient.

In *Wiser*, Sunstein and Hastie relate stories of Presidents Franklin D. Roosevelt and John F. Kennedy. Roosevelt would create devil's advocates by appearing to agree with advisers holding alternative views, thereby encouraging each to develop their views fully. He would then listen to the best overall arguments before making his decision. Kennedy appointed his brother Robert to the role of devil's advocate to prevent premature consensus. However, Sunstein and Hastie go on to explain that the research evidence does not support the appointment of black hat directors or devil's advocates, as the true value comes from authentic rather than orchestrated dissent.

> My advice is not to appoint a Chief Cynic. Instead, find a good facilitator and run a backcasting or pre-mortem exercise.

My advice is not to appoint a Chief Cynic. Instead, find a good facilitator and run a backcasting or pre-mortem exercise. Each is designed to look into a failed future and work backwards from there to determine what must have happened 'for us to be in this situation'. Once you have identified what happened, you can assess your ability to change your chosen course of action and/or to ensure you can avoid such a failure in future.

Chapter summary

This chapter explores different types of team leader roles in team decision making:

- The Chair of the Board needs to focus on a quality team to ensure the executive is able to provide high-quality information to the Board.
- The Commander-in-Chief must be very aware that what they say goes.
- Don't undervalue the role of Chief Risk Officer. They help you think things through.
- A Chief Safety Officer helps ensure psychological safety so staff speak up.
- Choose a good facilitator over a Chief Cynic such as a 'black hat director'.

13

Think like Einstein

Wouldn't we all like to be able to think like Einstein. Mind you, a quick google and you will find plenty of people pointing out the great man's failings.

Here I suggest you should think like Einstein because of one word: 'observer'. If you remember, in developing his special theory of relativity, Einstein developed a thought experiment involving a train, two bolts of lightning, an observer on the train and an independent observer standing on the platform.[45] I won't go into the thought experiment too far (if you want a refresher, you can always check out the video in the reference list).

For the observer on the moving train, the bolt of lightning at the front of the train occurs before the one at the rear of the train, as they are moving towards the light at the front and away from the light at the back. The independent observer on the platform sees the lightning hitting both front and rear simultaneously. The critical point for Einstein was that the two observers had a different frame of reference, which meant they saw different things.

In chapter 11 I took you through a series of models to help you lead a fruitful deliberation on a decision by the executive team that is as free of bias and noise as you can hope for. In *Noise*, Kahneman, Sibony and Sunstein suggest appointing a 'decision observer' to observe the discussion and point out, in real time, possible sources of bias and noise.

> It's a big call to appoint an independent observer to your executive team meeting, particularly for highly confidential and potentially game-changing discussions.

It's a big call to appoint an independent observer to your executive team meeting, particularly for highly confidential and potentially game-changing discussions. In fact, Kahneman et al. go on to say they prefer to recommend good decision hygiene, which is a term I have adopted for this last part of the book.

If you were to appoint a decision observer, and let's face it, some decisions are so important you want every card in the deck stacked in your favour, here are my recommendations. If you wish to go more broadly than my advice here, you'll find further tips listed in chapter 11 and in the appendix of *Noise*.

On appointing the observer:

- Don't delegate the role to an executive, and especially

not to the Chief Risk Officer, who, as noted in chapter 12, has a different role to play.
- If you don't want to go outside the company, consider a direct report to one of the executives, someone on the rise who will learn from the experience as well as have the confidence to speak up.

On the role of the observer:

- The chief role of the observer is to act as a circuit-breaker and restore balance to the conversation.
- They should not wait to interject when they see a possible causal factor of bias or noise.
- They should interject with a question, not an accusation — for example, 'Do we lack sufficient diversity for this decision?' Such a question might be asked when we are making decisions about young people. The answer might be on the level of consultation or market research conducted and fed into the discussion.

The observer should be trained to look for:

- *Diversity.* Is there the right mix of diverse backgrounds in the room, and what can be done to address any gaps?
- *Initiation.* How was the discussion initiated? (See the Think Model in chapter 11.)
- *Unshared.* Is everyone offering their opinion or just being agreeable?

- *Withheld.* Did the CEO ask if anyone has any other information that might be of interest to others concerning this decision?
- *Dissent.* Were any dissenting views suppressed, thereby damaging psychological safety?
- *Scales.* Are team members using subjective ratings, such as 'significant' or 'high', without a commonly agreed scale to define their meaning? The most obvious example is risk ratings without risk criteria; all such criteria should be objectively clarified.
- *Searched.* Did the team search for alternate explanations of what they are seeing or planning? This could be through research conducted before the discussion or through openly searching for information that could counter the current line of thinking.
- *Fatigue.* Is there evidence of fatigue among your people? They need to save their energy for decision making. Mark Zuckerberg knows this and reportedly wears the same clothes every day to reduce decision fatigue.[46]

Chapter summary

While experts call for a decision observer to help identify bias and noise in real time, I recommend that your Chief Risk Officer helps the team think things through.

The wrap

Thanks for accompanying me on this journey.

This is the third book in my trilogy on decision making: *Risky Business, Persuasive Advising, Team Think*. I'm passionate about decision making. Did that come through? My pursuit of excellence in decision making has naturally led me here.

Recognition of the importance of risk-based decision making arose in the later part of the last century, emerging from the behavioural sciences that proliferated in the second half of the twentieth century. Excellent books like Robert Cialdini's *Influence: The Psychology of Persuasion* drove research into the art of communicating to influence the decisions of others.

This century has seen a greater focus on team decision making. We all think our decision making is pretty good, and everyone else has a problem. What we need to understand is that if everyone else has a problem, then *we all* have a problem. That is how we make collective decisions as teams.

Where will the world take us next? I'm not sure. But as soon as I know the topic of my next book, I have a feeling I'll be able to give you a hint as to where we are heading with our thinking on improving decision making.

Given where the world is at as I finish the manuscript for *Team Think* in late 2023, with brutal wars in Gaza and Ukraine, increasingly vehement geopolitical discourse and polarised populations, we will need all the help we can get.

My plan, in the time I have left on this planet, is to develop as many high-performance leaders as I can who have advanced skills in leading team decision making. Maybe, just maybe, the shift in how teams make decisions will become self-sustaining, the number of high-performance leaders will grow and soon create a massive impact for the good of the world. For the sake of my kids and their kids, I certainly hope so.

If you would like to stay in touch and hear my developing thoughts on team decision making and topics related to team and organisational performance, please sign up to my blog at bryanwhitefield.com.

Endnotes

1. Galloway, Scott (2022); *Algebra of Decisions*, blog post 4 Feb. https://www.profgalloway.com/algebra-of-decisions/

2. Sunstein, Cass R, and Hastie, Reid (2014), *Wiser: Getting Beyond Groupthink to Make Groups Smarter*, chapter 2: Amplifying Errors.

3. Aminov, Iskandar, De Smet, Aminov, Jost, Gregor, and Mendelsohn, David (2019), *Decision making in the age of urgency*, McKinsey survey, April.

4. Nutt, Paul C (2002), *Why Decisions Fail: Avoiding the Blunders and Traps That Lead to Debacles*, Berrett-Koehler Publishers, San Francisco, CA.

5. Lovallo, D, and Sibony, O (2010), 'The Case for Behavioural Strategy', *McKinsey Quarterly*, March.

6. Kahneman, Daniel, and Lovallo, Don (2003), 'Delusions of Success: How Optimism Undermines Executives' Decisions', *Harvard Business Review*, pp. 1–10.

7. Smith, David J (2011), *Reliability, Maintainability and Risk*, 8th edn, Butterworth-Heinemann, Oxford, UK.

8. Janis, Irving L (1973), 'Groupthink and Group Dynamics: A Social Psychological Analysis of Defective Policy Decisions', *Policy Studies Journal*, 2(1), Sept 1.

9. Sunstein, Cass R, and Hastie, Reid (2014), *Wiser: Getting Beyond Groupthink to Make Groups Smarter*, Introduction — Beyond Groupthink.

10. Unknown origin according to the University of York, https://www.york.ac.uk/depts/maths/histstat/lies.htm (accessed 10 April 2023).

11. Bonabeau, Eric (2003), 'Don't Trust Your Gut, Decision Making and Problem Solving', *Harvard Business Review*, May, https://hbr.org/2003/05/dont-trust-your-gut

12. Kahneman, Daniel, Sibony, Olivier, and Sunstein, Cass R (2021), *Noise: A Flaw in Human Judgment*, Chapter 1: Crime and Noisy Punishment. Their reference: Danziger, Shai, Levav, Jonathan, and Avnaim-Pesso, Liora (2011),'Extraneous Factors in Judicial Decisions', *Proceedings of the National Academy of Sciences of the United States of America* 108(17), 6889–92

13. Kahneman, Daniel, Sibony, Olivier, and Sunstein, Cass R. (2021), *Noise: A Flaw in Human Judgment*, Chapter 2: A Noisy System.

14. Kahneman, Daniel, Sibony, Olivier, and Sunstein, Cass R. (2021), *Noise: A Flaw in Human Judgment*, Introduction: Two Kinds of Error.

15. Dignan, Aaron (2019), 'Changing Organizational Mindset', *Stanford Social Innovation Review*, March 18, https://ssir.org/books/excerpts/entry/changing_organizational_mindset

16. Price/earnings ratio is given by dividing the last sale

price by the average EPS (earnings per share) estimate for the specified fiscal time period. From: https://www.nasdaq.com/articles/whats-your-pe-ratio-analyst-blog-2013-08-13

17. Tatevosian, Parkev (2023), *If You'd Invested $10,000 in Facebook Stock in 2013, This Is How Much You Would Have Today*, The Motley Fool, March 17, https://www.nasdaq.com/articles/if-youd-invested-%2410000-in-facebook-stock-in-2013-this-is-how-much-you-would-have-today

18. Nemo, John (2014), 'What a NASA janitor can teach us about living a bigger life', *Denver Business Journal*, Dec. 23.

19. 'Mission statement', *The Economist*. Retrieved from: http://www.economist.com/ node/13766375

20. Converse, Sharolyn A, Cannon-Bowers, Janis A, and Salas, Eduardo (1991), 'Team Member Shared Mental Models: A Theory and Some Methodological Issues', *Proceedings of the Human Factors Society Annual Meeting*, 35(19): 5, Sep. 1.

21. Jeffery, Arthur B, Maes, Jeanne D, and Bratton-Jeffery, Mary F (2005), 'Improving team decision-making performance with collaborative modelling', *Team Performance Management* 11, no. ½, pp. 40–50.

22. Westli, Heidi Kristina, Johnsen, Bjørn Helge, Eid, Jarle, Rasten, Ingvil and Brattebø, Guttorm (2010), 'Teamwork skills, shared mental models, and performance in simulated trauma teams: an

independent group design', *Scandinavian Journal of Trauma, Resuscitation and Emergency Medicine* 18(47).

23. Flixborough (Nypro UK) explosion, 1 June 1974, Health and Safety Executive, UK, web page accessed 3 May 2023.

24. 'Self-made billionaires Richard Branson and Jeff Bezos reveal how they make tough decisions', CNBC.com, 2 March 2018. https://www.cnbc.com/2018/03/02/how-richard-branson-and-jeff-bezos-make-tough-decisions.html

25. Larson, Eric (2019), 'How Jeff Bezos Uses Faster, Better Decisions to Keep Amazon Innovating', *Forbes Magazine*, 24 Sept 2018, accessed 5 Dec. 2019.

26. Power, Daniel J., 'What is high-velocity decision making?', DSSResources.com

27. De Smet, Aaron, Lackey, Gerald, and Weiss, Leigh M (2017), 'Untangling your organization's decision making', *McKinsey Quarterly*, June 21, McKinsey.com

28. Power, Daniel J., 'What is high-velocity decision making?', DSSResources.com

29. Treynor, Jack L (1987), 'Market Efficiency and the Bean Jar Experiment', *Financial Analysts Journal* 43(3), 50–53, DOI: 10.2469/faj.v43.n3.50

30. Sigman, Mariano, and Ariely, Dan (2017), How can groups make good decisions?, TED Studio.

31. Sauro, Jeff (2016), Can you take the mean of ordinal data?, MeasuringU.

32. United Nations Treaty Collection, Chapter IV, 15 Human Rights.
33. Human Rights Watch, United States Ratification of International Human Rights Treaties.
34. Wikipedia, All Models are Wrong; https://en.wikipedia.org/wiki/All_models_are_wrong
35. From: http://www.smh.com.au/entertainment/tv-and-radio/88-20140122-317ff. html
36. From: http://www.australiaday.org.au/australia-day/history/1988-the-bicentenary/
37. From: http://www.australiaday.org.au/australia-day/history/1988-the-bicentenary, accessed 22 March 2015.
38. From https://www.who.int/health-topics/poliomyelitis#tab=tab_1, accessed 21 Dec. 2023.
39. Gates, Bill (2019), 'A bet on humanity worth every dollar', GatesNotes, September 20, accessed 22 Dec. 2023.
40. Bahar, H, Tan, FZ, and Altintas, F (2016), 'A Strategic Approach for Learning Organizations: Mental Models', 12th International Strategic Management Conference, ISMC 2016, 28–30 October 2016, Antalya, Turkey.
41. From https://thebulletin.org/doomsday-clock/, accessed 21 Dec. 2023.
42. Kissel, NH, and Foley, P (2019), 'The 3 Challenges Every New CEO Faces', *Harvard Business Review*, January 23, https://hbr.org/2019/01/the-3-challenges-every-new-ceo-faces

43. Belot, Henry (2018), 'ATO urges staff to dob in colleagues who take long lunches, read paper at work', February, www.abc.net.au

44. APRA Prudential Standard CPS 220 Risk Management.

45. 'Simultaneity — Albert Einstein and the Theory of Relativity, MyEarbot, YouTube channel, accessed 21 Dec. 2023.

46. Kim, Eugene (2014), 'Here's the Real Reason Mark Zuckerberg Wears the Same T-Shirt Every Day', *Inside Magazine*, Nov. 7, accessed 4 May 2023.

www.ingramcontent.com/pod-product-compliance
Lightning Source LLC
Chambersburg PA
CBHW052139070526
44585CB00017B/1892